Advanced E Methods

NMR, AFM, Arduino, Lithography

Thomas Gredig

California State University Long Beach

Title image: Atomic force microscopy image of phthalocyanine thin film; Gold circuit on glass created with InkJet printer photomask; Free induction decay curve for glycerine; Arduino micro controller board.

Email: mail@thomasgredig.com
Web: www.thomasgredig.com

Gredig, Thomas
    Advanced Experimental Methods
    NMR, AFM, Arduino, Lithography.
    First Edition.
    p. 144   6" x 9"
    Includes illustrations and bibliographical references.
    ISBN-13: 978-1975898120
    ISBN-10: 1975898125

Preface

EVERY student's education experience should include several laboratories. The laboratories not only convey hands-on experience, but provide important knowledge on ethics, lab notebook keeping, and literature review. This lab is intended for upper-division undergraduate, or early graduate students.

This accompanying lab book will not include the detailed processing steps included in a typical lab cookbook, or possibly undergraduate laboratory notebook. Rather, it aims at preparing you to perform a designed experiment with certain objectives. It is important that you understand the theoretical background of the experiment and you are encouraged to be curious and validate, test, and measure properties that go beyond the scope of this manual.

Four experimental techniques with broad applications are introduced, namely pulsed nuclear magnetic resonance, atomic force microscopy, optical photolithography, and the Arduino micro controller. You are also introduced to rigorous note taking, ethics, limited programming, data graphing, and report writing.

The structure of this manual is in chronological order of the labs, therefore you can read along as you perform the experiments. The experiments are preceded with information on ethical conduct, safety, scientific note taking, journal search, and lab report writing. In the next part, each of the four techniques is introduced with general theoretical background information. The experimentalist needs to throughly understand the equipment that he/she operates. In the second part, the four specific experiments are discussed. Each technique has two experiments listed, each of those experiments should take about 3 hours to complete. Included in the experimental section are also predictions. All predictions should be completed before you start the experiment and recorded in the lab notebook. The predictions are in place of a hypothesis that researchers make before completing the experiment. The predictions will help you with the analysis part of the report.

This laboratory was first developed in 2008 at California State University Long Beach in order to prepare Master's degree students for experimental research with the specific aim to foster the scientific method applied to modern physical experimentation, and to understand how to present results to the scientific audience both in oral presentations as well as written form.

Since the introduction of the course, many students have participated, both graduate and undergraduate students, all of whom have contributed in some way to what has been included in this booklet.

Thomas Gredig

First Edition, August 28, 2017

Contents

1 Advanced Physics Lab

> The principle of science, the definition almost, is the following: The test of all knowledge is experiment. Experiment is the sole judge of scientific truth. But what is the source of knowledge? Where do the laws that are to be tested come from? Experiment, itself, helps to produce these laws, in the sense that it gives us hints.
>
> *Richard Feynman*

1.1 Goals

THE "Experimental Methods" class is a unique opportunity to experience physics through exploration. In essence, you will be able to test knowledge and make physical predictions to pre-determine outcomes. You will do this in an organized manner. A good experimenter uses a methodical approach. Therefore, it is important to be apply consistent word attitudes and practice the organizational steps in order to build expertise. In the following, we provide you with 4 experiments and one open-ended project. This will give you repetitive practice with the goal to hone your skills towards expert level.

For each experiment, start with a scientific question and apply a systematic approach. Then, you will do some reading on background information; some information is available herein, but there are many other resources online, especially journals and articles that review the topic. The predictions need to be completed before you begin you experiment as a part of your proposal. Next, you will be able to craft one or more hypotheses that you can then experimentally test. When you execute the experiment, it is important that you are skeptical, constantly make checks and validations, and carefully note all parameters. These parameters are recorded in the lab notebook. For scientists, details are very important and often the primary source for new developments, ideas, and important results. A common myth is perpetuated that new scientific discoveries only happen in leading labs with state-of-the-art equipment, when it is probably more accurate to say that discoveries come from persistent experimentation with a keen eye on details. Hence, a good background in the field and a good lab record are tremendously useful.

If the procedure is not working properly, you will have to troubleshoot. This is an important part to the experiment. You will also build instrumental expertise to expand your curriculum vitae.

The recorded data that comes directly from the machine / equipment will be referred to as *raw data*. It is important to save all raw data securely. It is a mandate to keep it unaltered. There is a specific procedure to label raw data files, which are detailed in Sec. 3.1.1.

The raw data is converted to graphs, which are called results. You should graph all results and add captions. Most researchers will print some results and keep them in the lab notebook as well. Next, the results are analyzed, transformed, normalized, and compared with the predictions and hypothesis. This step is referred to as the analysis.

Finally, the experimenter determines whether the hypothesis was true or false and whether agreement with the prediction was obtained. Often this process leads towards new ideas, testable hypotheses, and extensions of the experiment.

1.1.1 Course Goals

Everyone will be able to engage, design, and test several physical concepts that are universally used. The course goals can be summarized as follows:

- Demonstrate mathematical and conceptual understanding of nuclear magnetic resonance, atomic force microcopy, micro controllers, electronic sensors and photolithography,
- analyze and evaluate scientific hypotheses using experiments,
- demonstrate ability to write and speak critically about lab experiments,

- effectively communicate results verbally and in writing,
- conduct laboratories ethically and keep scientific notebooks,
- design an experiment, apply a model, evaluate, and present the results, and
- write lab reports based on scientific writing patterns.

This experience surely broadens your skill set, makes available tools for your immediate research, helps with data analysis, and extends your curriculum vitae. The laboratory enables the connection between the experimental data, model systems and fundamental theories. Strong collaborative skills are necessary to produce documents and work together on projects. Such collaborations are vital and important to develop successful careers in science. As a theoretician, you learn details on how to interpret and understand experimental data, and as an experimentalist you receive training to efficiently conduct experiments.

You will write the Standard Operating Procedure (SOP) as a team. You will also perform the experiment, and do the data collection as a team. However, you will write individual lab reports. A final project will allow you to be creative and conclude the course with the design of your own experiment. Finally, you can present the content. The final project should deepen your understanding of one of the learned experimental equipments and leverage it imaginatively for exploration.

1.2 Tools

In order to conduct research effectively, you will need to aggregate skills to know tools. We will familiarize you with a standard approach and some specific tools. The reading alone will not be sufficient, but you will need to actively engage with them. In terms of software, we base our choice on the following criterion, the tool should be (a) open source and freely available, (b) available on multiple platforms, (c) have extensions and large user base. A brief summary of the tools is provided in the order that you should approach them and references to sections with more details are made.

- Research article database: IOP Science database, Web of Science, Google Scholar (Section 4.2)
- Reference manager: Zotero (Section 4.4.1)
- Data repository for raw data: Dropbox (Section 3.1)

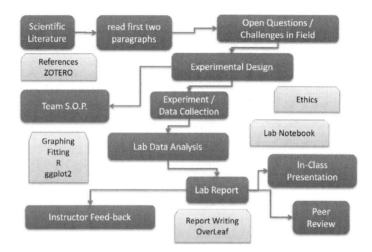

Figure 1.1: Typical process for experiments involves search of important research papers in the scientific literature. The open questions and challenges in the field are generally discussed in the first few paragraphs. This leads to an experimental design to explore the open questions and challenges. A standard operation procedure (SOP) is created to reproduce the experimental procedure when needed. The experiment is conducted and the data is collected and afterwards analyzed. The results and analysis are summarized in a lab report and presented. The report generally receives feed-back from peers and supervisor.

- Graphing data: RStudio and R (Section 4.10) based ggplot2
- Lab report templates: LaTeX(Section 4.5) on OverLeaf.com or ShareLatex.com
- Data analysis: NIH ImageJ (Fig. 7.5), Gwyddion, WSxM, R (Section 4.10)
- Bibliography: BibTeX (Section 4.4)

Whenever your research topic changes, you need to familiarize yourself with the current state of the art in the chosen field. To do so, you will use search databases and you may use a systematic approach detailed elsewhere.(Miller et al., 2009) The databases are either available through the library or Google Scholar service. For physics, the library suggests to use the IOP Science database, the advanced search of the AIP Scitation service, or the Web of Science. Alternatively, you can use the LANL physics preprint service (`arxiv.org`) from Cornell University or the advanced option in Google Scholar. If you are using Google Scholar, you should go to "Settings" and "Library Links" and add "CSU Long Beach", so that links to the full articles are made available through the CSU Long Beach subscription service.

Once you have found articles, collect the article in your database and save them with Zotero, following the activity in Section 4.4.1. Best practice includes systematic naming convention, for example, it is suggested to name files author.lastname_title.firstword_year. An example would be *gredig_ control_ 2010.pdf* for reference Gredig, Gentry, Colesniuc, and Schuller (2010).

Other tools that are important to be familiar with include:

- Oscilloscope (Section 9.1)
- Micro-controller: controlling and reading sensors (Section 8.4)
- Hot plate (Section 7.3.5)
- Diamond scribe: cutting, cleaving substrates (Section 7.3.2)

If you are unsure on how to operate any of the tools, seek help from peers, the instructor, and always carefully read the manuals before use of new instruments.

1.3 Ethical and Legal Considerations

What is ethics in the Sciences? Ethical behavior has a long tradition in science and is necessary for its continuation. Misconduct in science centers around reporting research results that are fabricated, plagiarized, and or falsified, see http://www.aps.org/programs/education/ethics/ (Kirby & Houle, 2004). Appropriate conduct includes

- proper record-keeping;
- truthful, careful handling and reporting of data;
- responsible, respectful interactions with peers and subordinates;
- adherence to journal publication guidelines, including proper recognition of research contributions.

We can use some basic rules from sociologist Robert Merton (1910 – 2003) who is known for his work on "unintended consequences". The Mertonian norms provide a guide for doing scientific research (Macfarlane & Cheng, 2008). Using the mnemonic CUDOS, the scientific principles should follow **Communalism, Universalism, Disinterestedness, Originality, and Skepticism**.

Communalism means that research, results, and information should be available publicly. Open access journals and archives (http://arxiv.org) provide some of those resources in physics. The second principle supports the notion that anyone - regardless of race, culture, nationality, or gender - can and should participate. The scientific pursuit is designed not to benefit personal interest, but to help the common scientific enterprise as understood through disinterestedness. Scientific results can be reproduced and verified by other teams; this is an intrinsic property. The disinterestedness has been mentioned as a reason for low rates of fraud in science.(Merton, 1996) What sets scientific research apart from the colloquial word of *search* or *research* is that it contributes something new, extends the current understanding through a process called originality. Scientific claims should be exposed to scrutiny before they are accepted. This skeptical part and utter objective scrutiny should be part of a scientist. The last step is called the review process. Young scientists must be trained in all these five aspects.

Research involving human subjects - especially physics education research - always requires an institutional review board (IRB), and independent ethics committee, to approve the work before it is undertaken. In that case, the participant population must first be identified, then permission from the IRB is obtained. Next, the research information must be presented to the participants and withdrawal at any time made available, also questions must be answered by participant. After giving

6

participants time to consider, a signed consent must be obtained before research can start.

1.3.1 APS Guidelines for Professional Conduct

The American Physical Society publishes the *APS Guidelines for Professional Conduct* (`https://www.aps.org/policy/statements/02_2.cfm`) with the goal to advance and diffuse the knowledge of physics. In summary, the research data must be stored and retained for a reasonable period of time. For publication, selection of data cannot be used; this may mislead or deceive the readership. Theft of data from others is also interdicted. **Plagiarism constitutes unethical scientific behavior and is never acceptable.** What constitutes as plagiarism is sometimes clear, and sometimes more complex. For complex cases, different web resources, including the CSULB library resources, are available, see `http://csulb.libguides.com/infoethics`, and its copyright information at `http://web.csulb.edu/library/reserve/copyright.html`.

Sometimes, it makes sense to add existing figures and graphs to a lab report or presentation. In these cases, it is important not to infringe on any copyright laws. The owner of a figure, graph, or image has the exclusive right to allow reproduction of the work. Therefore, unless the creator has explicitly stated that the work is free to use, it cannot be used without permission. The only exception is "fair use", which can be difficult to understand. Lab reports generally qualify as original work, so they cannot use any figures or graphs without explicit permission. For presentations, the educational aspect of "fair use" can be incorporated, which allows certain reproduction with clear markings showing the source of the work at the bottom of the slide. Never, it is allowed to give the impression that the work is one's own. If a particular figure needs to be include, it is possible to make one's own graph based on the data available and then reference the original work that produced the data.

When publishing, reporting data, it is important to list contributions. Significant contributors need to be listed as co-authors, others need to be acknowledged. It is the author's obligation to promptly retract and correct errors in published work. Peer review is critical to the scientific endeavor, the reviewers have privileged access to information and ideas, which must be kept confidential. Any conflicts of interests must be disclosed.

Collaborators share some degree of responsibility for the authenticity of the published work. The research data and work must be accurate and verifiable. In collaborations, a process to archive data and communication must be in place.

Authors have an obligation to their peers and the entire science community to include references that communicate the precedents, sources and context of the reported work. Credit must be given, deliberate omission is unethical and unacceptable.

Here are the four criteria for authorship on a refereed journal or publication. (1) You should make substantial contributions (design of work, acquisition, analysis, interpretation), and (2) help draft the work and (3) approve the publication and (4) agree to be accountable for all aspects of the work. If contributors do not fulfill all 4 criteria, they can be listed in the acknowledgements. Authorship is not deserved for (a) grant acquisition, general supervision, (c) writing assistance or proofreading. The American Physical Society states that acknowledgements imply endorsement, therefore written permission to be acknowledged is required from all parties. In condensed matter physics, the first author is generally the main contributor, followed by additional authors with decreasing contributions, and the last author listed is the research group leader (usually a professor). High energy physics journals use alphabetical listings.

1.3.2 Copyright

The United States of America has a copyright law, which governs reproduction of work. Work that you create is automatically copyrighted. You are not allowed to use other's work unless you have their permission. Much work that is available on the internet is copyrighted and cannot be used in lab reports, or thesis work, for example, unless there is a license that permits reproduction.

Researchers generally transfer the copyrights to the journals. When a researcher creates a figure, then this figure belongs to the researcher. When he or she publishes the work, now the figure's rights are transferred to the journal. If the researcher decides to include that same figure in his/her thesis, written permission to publish must be obtained from the journal unless the transfer copyright forms said otherwise. If the figure is substantially re-graphed and re-purposed, it can be included in the thesis or dissertation.

The copyright law allows *fair use*, i.e. you may reproduce specific portions with references.

Inevitably, some findings in research lead to inventions that might lead to patents. Patents are different from copyright and generally involve a specific design, process, machine, or composition of matter. The researcher should be aware that employers and universities have regulations, restrictions, and procedures in place for patenting. Generally, the patent should be filed before submitting an article to a journal for publication.

1.4 Outcomes

What outcomes can you expect from this text and the related experimental work? For one, you will learn to systematically conduct experiments, using the ethos of science, the methodology of notebook keeping, and following the safety rules. For each experiment, you will apply the concepts and basic models based on the theoretical understanding. You will operate the tools and write a Standard Operating Procedure (SOP) that enables anyone to run the experimental process following the succinct logical steps of that outline. The results from each experiment are summarized and analyzed in a laboratory report that closely resembles the format of research publications. Some of the experimental work is presented to an audience giving you experience in communication as well. In the final step, you will get to apply all steps to design your own experiment for the final project.

2 Safety

THE experimental lab requires that you learn about safety and strictly comply with all safety regulations and standards. Chemicals used in this lab may be dangerous and you agree to read the materials safety datasheet (MSDS) before using any chemical. In the lithography lab, you need to wear safety goggles to protect your eyes from splashes as well as UV radiation. You also need to wear a gown to protect your clothes, as well as appropriate protective gloves for handling chemicals. Additionally,

- wear closed shoes and pants, sandals and short skirts or shorts are not permitted,
- wear safety goggles when handling chemicals and being exposed to UV radiation,
- store chemicals in designed storage areas and handle them inside the fume hood,
- never work in the laboratory unless the instructor is present,
- do not perform experiments that are not authorized by the instructor,
- dispose chemicals, and glass products in special containers that are explicitly labeled,
- always verify that the ultra-sonic bath is filled with enough distilled water,
- never remove the sample from the AFM without raising the head well above the sample,
- always apply ultra care, when approaching the sample with an AFM tip,
- immediately turn off the NMR, if it starts to beep, or overheat,
- label everything,
- not bring any drinks or food items into the lab, since they are not permitted

Your instructor will show you the safety shower and the eyewash, which must be used for at least 15 minutes in the event of an emergency.

Please note that glassware cannot be discarded into the regular trash. Also, wipes that have been contaminated with photoresist need to be disposed of properly. Each waste container must be clearly labeled for the waste product. The start date of first waste collection is noted and cannot exceed 6 months. An instructor should be informed before the six month expiration date is reached, so that trained people can take proper care of the waste. No overfilling can occur as this can also be a safety issue. Liquids cannot be mixed.

In addition to these general rules for safety, please carefully review the safety procedures for each of the experiments.

For the atomic force microscopy, never move the head, while the cantilever is imaging, engaged, or close to the surface. For the electronics, it is important the computer is always on, if the controller is on. Don't unplug hardware, first turn it off, then you can unplug. Most importantly, if you are unsure, then ask.

3 Scientific Lab Notebook

Dans les champs de
l'observation le hasard ne
favorise que les esprits
préparés – In the fields of
observation chance favours
only the prepared mind.

Louis Pasteur

A N integral part of any research lab is the *lab notebook*. Here, research
refers to independent investigations as opposed to searching and
reading work that has been conducted elsewhere. In this course, we
will use notebooks in a similar way that scientists use them. For the
purpose of this course the notebook can be an inexpensive composition
book with 80 sheets, 9.75" x 7.5" in size, for example. It must be a
bound notebook for reasons detailed below. The type of paper used in
a notebook is often also important. Acid-free paper will not deteriorate
over time as fast as regular wood-based paper and it should not turn
yellow.

Professional scientists use the lab notebook to record events, such
as experimental methods, file names, calculations, diagrams, sketches,
ideas (creativity), suggestions, plans, observations, links, emails from
collaborators, important plots and graphs, summaries, and abstracts,
and important events.

Beyond that, the notebook provides a way to disseminate one's own
ideas deliberately. It can be thought of as a thinking tool to help
fortify the thinking process. It also encourages writing, a skill that is
strengthened by frequent practice. Sketching ideas, making drawings
and diagrams is an essential part in the notebook. Visualization of
ideas is an important aspect of communication and fosters collaboration
between peers and teachers. In the end, the notebook will become an
integral tool for writing reports, articles, and formulating a complete
thesis. The lab notebook provides the historical (temporal) perspective,

while a lab report, poster, presentation, or publication portray the logical flow of events. d

3.1 Organization

The organization of the lab notebook takes some practice. Here, the most basic structural elements for keeping a scientific notebook are summarized (Kanare, 1985).

All pages in the notebook need to be numbered; also set page numbers apart from other numbers by encircling them; no page can be left completely empty - write "intentionally left empty" to fill any such page. You should keep close records of the dates and even the times in the day in some cases. Notebooks and log books should have a longevity of about 30 years or more. Therefore, use pens and paper that resist degradation. Use water, acids, and other common lab chemicals to try to wash off writing in order to test for the best pen to use. The notebook should also be bound (not spiral or loose-leaf), otherwise there is a chance that pages are removed or inserted. Pencils are not allowed, anything that can be erased leads to ethical problems. White-out cannot be used; only cross-outs are allowed, such that the text underneath is still legible.

The first two pages should be reserved for *"Table of Contents"* and *"Projects"* which you update with time and include the page numbers and date in three separate columns. Also make sure to include complete contact information, such that the notebook can be returned in the event that it goes missing.

Penmanship is crucial. The writing must be legible, clear, and each section needs a concise, descriptive heading. Headings include *"Purpose"*, *"Method"*, *"Experiment"*, *"Analysis"*, *"Apparatus"*, ... and should be used to delineate different parts.

Use acid-free glue or high-quality tape to insert paper snippets, printouts, graphs, and other data into the lab notebook. The historical order is not interrupted. If the graph cannot be added at the moment, when the data is recorded, then no space should be kept for it. Rather at the later point in time, when it is added, the graph is pasted in the new empty space with a reference to the page number of when the raw data was collected.

Lab notebooks generally stay inside the lab and belong to the research laboratory. The lab notebook is separate and specific to each lab. It belongs to the lab director, who can inspect and verify the notebook periodically. The lab notebook should be stored safely.

Dates need to be recorded clearly (10/13/12 is not clear). The year always needs to be included using the full 4-digit representation. The month can be spelled out, if it is ambivalent. Due to data saving and ordering on computers, the recommended format is yyyy-mm-dd, or year-month-day representation.

Bad record keeping can have ill effects. In the worst case of disputes, credit of discoveries cannot be given.

The data is crucial to an experimenter and absolute and outmost care needs to be taken in collecting and storing scientific data. Data that is stored on computers must comply with a data management plan. This is a formal document that describes the process of securing and organizing lab data. It is a requirement for many grants, such as National Science Foundation (NSF), Department of Energy (DOE), or Department of Defense (DoD).

Data includes measurement points gathered using equipment, software programs, models, reports, and publications. If the data is stored in proprietary formats, it can cause problems at a later time. First of all, some formats may no longer be supported or become outdated. They may be operating system dependent. As a general rule, data should be stored in text format, preferred format is CSV (comma separated files) or if the data is more complex in XML. The format (metadata) needs to be documented; i.e. the files should include consistent headers with units in one line and possibly follow a strict convention. If data is acquired in a compressed or proprietary format, it must be converted to text format and stored along with the original data. The procedure of data conversion is part of the data management plan.

3.1.1 File Naming Convention

Slightly different conventions exist between labs. However, best practice suggests that all raw data files are stored in one single folder called RAW in a flat format (there are no sub-folders). Therefore, the file names ought to be unique. The generation of unique file names is as follows. Each raw data file name contains 6 parts: **(1)** the recording date (yyyymmdd-), **(2)** the project name, **(3)** the instrument name, **(4)**, the main user's initials, **(5)** the sample name, and **(6)** extra description.

An example would be `20140820-nmrlab-PNMR-tg-GL01-run1`. In this case the sample name is `GL01` and the author's initials are `tg`. The file name needs to be recorded in the lab notebook and the extension depends on the machine. In this fashion, one RAW folder contains all data files and they can easily be searched by date. In fact, if you look at your notebook, you should almost be able to guess the filename from for the experiment performed on a certain date. Alternatively, you could easily search for all files that belong to the project called `nmrlab` or all files from sample `GL01`. Typical instrument names include `PNMR` for pulsed nuclear magnetic resonance, `AFM` for atomic force microscopy, and `XRD` for x-ray diffractometer.

3.1.2 Notebook Organization

What are some good examples and traits of a successful lab notebook? It should include some of the following *ingredients*:

- personal expressions, comments ("good sample", "worked well", "process is too long", etc.)
- sketches, drawings, diagrams, processes
- questions, predictions, and hypotheses
- full sentences with reflections and analysis
- detailed descriptions of the experimental procedure

Many lab notebook keepers will also sign the page at check-out, or have the notebook inspected and signed by the lab supervisor.

You should acquire a style of notebook keeping that avoids making notes on loose paper, only to be recopied later. Your style of record keeping should be useful to others, therefore use legible writing, and complete accounts of your experimental procedure and details. For computer programs, include flow diagrams in your notebook. Keep your notebook in a well-protected space. Keep your audience in mind. For one, it will be yourself, you will want to write a lab report or thesis based on the measured results. Another person may be a peer who will continue measurements. Clarity in writing is important, some details may be clear at the moment, but will be in question later in time. It must be recorded to avoid confusion later on.

All information and data must be recorded unambiguously. Describe the conditions of the laboratory. Flexibility in the format should be used, however. Always include the leading 0 for numbers < 1.

3.2 Evaluation

The evaluation rubric of the lab notebook is based on the following criteria:

1. full name and department on cover

2. start date (and end date if full) on cover

3. first page: complete contact information, including email

4. second page: table of contents (will be filled in with time)

5. date and times are recorded, if other people helped take data, include their names

6. all pages are numbered; page numbers are circled

7. no pages are skipped (blank)

8. all dates are spelled out in format yyyy-mm-dd (include 4-digit year and order in this way)

9. use only pens (no pencils, white-out) that withstand water, alcohol stains and withstand time

10. use headers, organize whenever possible

11. include appropriate sections such as "pupose", "method", "results"

12. include complete record of experiments, use full sentences

13. include every filename of data that is recorded, or for programs that you write

14. filenames should be unique (NOT experiment1.dat or test5.dat) and in accordance with section 3.1

15. if graphs are taped, make sure they are well-taped, no post-its, loose paper

16. mistakes are never blacked-out or deleted with white-out, rather crossed-through, or if occurred in the past amended with a note (referring to the current page, where the corrected information is given)

In the event, that you discover, that past data was recorded incorrectly, make the amendments on the new pages (current time) and only add a reference to the current page number on the old pages. Do not change the past.

3.3 Notebook Examples

The content and organization between lab notebooks varies a lot. In fact, notebooks have personal and distinct character. You may also have seen bad examples, incomplete lab notebooks. Therefore, it is important to self-review the notebook, based on the organization and evaluation principles outlined in sections 3.1 and 3.2. It makes sense to also read and study notebooks from other scientists (Kanare, 1985).

One famous scientist from the 19th century was **Charles R. Darwin** (1809 – 1882). His best known book is called "On the Origin of Species" (1859), in which he rejects some earlier concepts on transmutation of species. In the book, Darwin describes his voyage around the world and explains the origin of species through natural selection. He kept notebooks in order to keep track of events. Many of his notebooks are available online (`http://darwin-online.org.uk/`). A typical notebook was leather-bound and contained about 100 folios (leaf), effectively 200 pages. The table of contents was added to the front page for archival purposes. It was written in ink. In the text, Darwin states facts from other scientists and debates them in the text. He uses words such as "to my view" and questions like "Why would we have . . . ". The Edinburgh notebook (1827) contains a lot of sketches. Darwin's notebook B is particularly famous as it shows sketches between related species corresponding to the tree of life.

An extensive library of books exists for physicist **Marie Curie** (1867 – 1934) chronicling her life. She was awarded the Nobel Prize in physics for her discovery of radium. A few years later, she received a second Nobel prize in Chemistry. She was a brilliant and determined scientist, born in Poland, and worked in France. Her notebooks are kept in lead-boxes, since they are radioactively contaminated. Radium has a half-life of 1600 years after all. Notes over a three-year period from 1899 are available in the Wellcome Library in London. It contains notes of experiments on radio-active substances, and pen-drawings of the apparatus. Madame Curie included notes on setting up equipment, experimental conditions, and nice drawings of how electrical wires were connected. She also kept nice tables that interrupted the flow of text and equipment sketches. Interestingly, she noted strange observations – on thorium oxide activity decreasing with air flow in the ionization chamber - which were not published. Rutherford, a bit later, found the same and postulated the emission of radioactive gas by thorium oxide. She used lines to delineate experiments and separate portions.

Physicist **Albert Einstein** (1879 – 1955) known for his publications on special and general relativity kept good notebooks. The notebooks are available at `http://alberteinstein.info/gallery/science.html`. One notebook is particularly famous, it is the Zürich notebook written in 1912 – 1913, it contains both images, equations, sketches, and words. This notebook - subtitled "Notes for lecture on Relativity" - describes the fruitful phase of Einstein towards developing the general relativity (Straumann, 2011). Note the page numbers are centered at the bottom of each page and surrounded by dashes, so that they are not confused with any numbers. He used dividing lines to separate parts. On page 38, he writes "lautet unsere Nebenbedingung", which is interesting because he uses the word "unsere" (our) to discuss his own work. In this case, "we" corresponds to the "royal I". Einstein used notebooks to jot down tidy and messy notes, some notes have annotations, some pages include calculations and some pages are crossed out, followed by "Nochmalige Berechnung" (Zürich notebook, p. 37) or new calculation. Most of the notes were not intended to be read by others (Janssen et al., 2007).

Another Nobel laureate who kept nice lab notebooks is chemist **Linus Pauling** (1901 – 1994). His notebooks are available online (`http://scarc.library.oregonstate.edu/coll/pauling/rnb/`); a total of 46 notebooks are available and the handwriting is particularly legible. He includes references to literature in his notebook. In the writing you find words that express his emotions, such as "a beautiful hemochromogen spectrum" (July 9, 1935). These words are perfectly acceptable in a personal research notebook, and give away success and failure, however, they are not to be used in publications or lab reports, where the text is devoid of emotional words. Indeed, the lab notebook is a subjective account that is translated into an objective narrative to be published. You may also note that times are included, such as "10 AM Sunday January 19, 1936" (Notebook 13, p. 47). In another example, you can see that Pauling singly and doubly underlines words to provide content. He also uses headers such as "Discussion" and indents paragraphs. You note on page 49, he writes "See p. 113 for correction". The practice with notebooks is to provide a historical account, therefore corrections cannot and must not be added to past pages. At one point, he writes "I have no explanation to this to offer.", which is a complete sentence rather than some shorthand.

Finally, physicist **Richard Feynman** (1918 – 1988) is known for his teaching style and contributions to quantum electrodynamics. Some of Feynman's notes are available in the Caltech archives (`http://archives.caltech.edu/`). His notebooks contain lots of diagrams and sketches, ultimately culminating in what we know as Feynman diagrams. His idea of the notebook is that it slowly grows the knowledge from something fuzzy into something concrete. That demands sometimes an ability to focus and deliberately add careful notes over longer periods. It is another skill to practice, if you fully embrace and accept the benefits of notebook keeping.

In summary, these accounts show examples of lab notebook taking. In particular, you learned that full sentences are used in conjunction with date and time stamps, and header lines. Often, it is a subjective account with a personal style. The lab notebook plays an important role for any scientist, it protects the owner from (legal) disputes by keeping records and original work safe.

3.4 Trends

Scientific note taking has changed over time. In earlier times (17th century), some notes (Gallilei) were encrypted or distributed as anagrams to claim first authorship, but not to give away all ideas. Before typewriters, notebooks served the important task of organizing thoughts. More recently, electronic note-taking has taken foot hold (Giles, 2012). Some researchers are using shared document spaces, such as offered by Google or through Dropbox. More specific solutions include LabGuru (biology oriented) or Quartzy (`https://www.quartzy.com/`). For large collaboration such tools may become important, although it is clear that they create an overhead, backup issues, extra costs, flexibility, and require maintenance by a supervisor. Still, taking notes in a acid-free notebook is common and standard practice and maintains the most advantages over long periods of time.

4 Scientific Research Papers

You will learn to read, write, and understand scientific publications, including research papers, dissertations, and M.S. theses. It turns out there are basic patterns that research papers generally follow. By reading scientific papers, you will become familiar with this specific structure. Writing reports allows you some practical experience with this style.

4.1 Literature Search

Science is an ever-evolving process. In order to start, you will need to obtain some background information about what experiments have been completed most recently and which theoretical models have been proposed and tested. There are many journals that publish results. The wealth of available articles may make it difficult for someone new to a field to find relevant information.

There is a procedure, which is detailed in an article by Miller et al. (2009). It starts off by using a journal database. These journal databases are listed by the library under the subject. There are several websites that can be helpful in locating research articles:

- http://iopscience.iop.org/search
- http://scitation.aip.org/
- http://arxiv.org/
- http://isiknowledge.com/
- http://scholar.google.com/

In order to narrow your field, you may target specific journals, specific search engines, and relevance sorting. All three will be briefly described here. You may start your search in a specific journal. For the physical sciences a few peer-reviewed journals are the following:

- Physical Review Letters (PRL)
- Physical Review A,B,C,D,E (PRA,PRB,PRC,PRD,PRE)
- Applied Physics Letters (APL)

- Journal of Applied Physics (JAP)
- Reviews of Modern Physics (RMP)
- Europhysics Letters (EPL)
- Nanoletters
- Physics Today

The importance of a journal is generally denoted by an index called *impact factor*, a higher impact factor means more relevance. The impact factor of a journal may change yearly. The impact factor of PRL is 7.3 (2009) and the impact factor PRB is 3.5 (2009), for example. At first, it is suggested to read *"review papers"* that give an overview of the topic and often cite important literature. You can then continue reading papers that are cited in this review article.

Expert readers in physics often read a journal article not in a linear fashion, but start by reading the title, the authors, affiliations, and the abstract. If the interest is awakened, then they quickly turn to the figures and read all the captions. Next, the expert readers often take a quick look at the summary or conclusive remarks, before turning to other content in the paper. The first and sometimes the first two paragraphs give you a review of previous work and motivations for the research. Therefore, as a part of the literature review process, after finding papers, focus on reading the first paragraph after the abstract and take notes of the motivation for the research.

If you begin reading articles, you should steer to the first two paragraphs. These paragraphs summarize the motivation for the specific background. Open questions and puzzles are often raised in these important paragraphs. Using pen and paper, find about 10 articles on a chosen topic and only read the first 2 paragraphs, then summarize the motivation for each article. You should get a good perspective quickly.

4.2 Search Strategies

When entering a new field with a vast repository of journal articles and information, a strategy must be applied to find informative, reliable, and broad articles in the new field. Database engines can be used for this purpose. Always use the *"advanced search"* option, either in Google Scholar or Web Of Science searches. If you are unfamiliar with a topic and want to find out what has been published in this field, then start a search using the topic search field **TS**. For example, **TS=atomic force microscopy**, then sort your search by most citations. The most cited work generally can be viewed as being perceived as more relevant by the research community. Scan the 10 to 20 most cited works in the field and combine reoccurrences in the title. Then refine your search by limiting the journals, for example. Useful fields to refine your search are the title field **TI**, the published year field **PY**, or the journal **SO**. If you are interested in articles on nanotubes from CSULB, you could search for **TS=nanotubes AND ZP=90840**, for example. An article published in Physical Review Letters will be general and more readable than a more narrow journal. Sort again for most cited, or most recent articles. Once you find a few intriguing titles, read the introductions of several related papers while taking notes. At this point you should have general idea of the questions that arise in the field. Use this additional data to focus your searches and create a better picture of the research field and how to position your work within.

Several tools can be used for a reference manager. A simple tool is the add-on for Chrome browser called Zotero, which can also run as a stand-alone application. It easily integrates with LibreOffice Writer and LaTeXdocuments.

4.3 LaTeX

Most professional publishers use a compiler to create documents. Most commonly, this compiler is based on a language called LaTeX. Unlike traditional Word processing software, it is not a WYSIWYG (what you see is what you get) software. The idea is that the program takes care of all the formatting and you are solely responsible for the text and the graphs. Therefore, if you were to write a report, you could easily compile it one way (two-column format), and then compile it for another publishing style (double-spaced document). Often you will write several reports, so that you only need to worry about the formatting once; you can instead focus on the content more as you progress. Moreover, the compiler takes care of labeling figures, positioning figures, and referencing / citing.

Most physicists are familiar with LaTeXand it is standard on Mac OS. The most common distribution is called MikTeX (`http://miktex`

.org/) and can be installed on other operating systems. Additionally, an editor is used. For Windows, the editor that is preferred is called WinShell (http://www.winshell.de/), and for Mac OS it is TeXShop (http://pages.uoregon.edu/koch/texshop/). Since the installation may be troublesome for some users, there is an online version, which requires no installation and maintenance at all, called OverLeaf (https://www.overleaf.com/). In that case, you can register using your email. OverLeaf also makes many report templates available, so that you can quickly start with your report.

4.3.1 Getting Started with LaTeX

In OverLeaf, after login, you create a NEW PROJECT. You can select a "blank" project or choose a template. You will have a split screen, on the left are the files for the document, in the middle, you find the code, and on the right side is the compiled document, which you can download in PDF. Each LaTeXdocument has two sections, namely a header and the document. In the header, you include the definitions, usually, you don't change anything after loading the template. The second part starts after \begin{document}, see Lst. 4.1. Your text can simply be inserted after the command \section{Introduction} and before \end{document}. If you start with a blank document, or use your own compiler, then the code in listing 4.1 will be a good starting point.

Use the \section{} command to generate title headings, which are automatically numerated. If you want to avoid the numbering, then add * after the word \section, such as \section*{Introduction}.

Physicists and mathematicians particularly use equations, which are easily typeset using dollar signs. The dollar signs surround the mathematical text and also parameters, so that they are cursive in the text. For example, an RC circuit would have the time-dependent electric potential $V(t)$ typeset by $V_0 e^{-t /(RC)}$ which shows as $V_0 e^{-t/(RC)}$. As you can see, the underscores create subscripts, and carrots are used for superscripts. The curly brackets define, which part to superset. Use \sin \theta for functions to display $\sin \theta$ and note the slash for the sine function. Without the slash it would not be a function, but the product of three variables.

Listing 4.1: The following sample code shows a typical lab report wrapper. In order to make the report double-spaced, simple replace the *reprint* in the documentclass to *preprint*.

```
\documentclass[aps,prb,amsmath,amssymb,reprint]{revtex4-1}
\usepackage{graphicx}

\begin{document}
\title{My Title}
\author{Your Name}
\affiliation{Department of Physics and Astronomy,
California State University Long Beach, CA 90840}
\date{\today}

\maketitle

\section*{Introduction}
Your Text
\bibliographystyle{plain}
\bibliogrpahy{myBib}

\end{document}
```

In Lst. 4.1, the document class is RevTeX, which includes many useful macros for the Physical Review journals. One such macro is useful to include an abstract. You simply surround the abstract with \begin{abstract} and \end{abstract}, and it will be formatted properly. The same can be done with the acknowledgement. Towards the end of the document, use \begin{acknowledgement} and the corresponding end command.

If you have not compiled a document in LaTeX, try to compile Listing 4.1 in OverLeaf, omit the \bibliography for now, as it will be explained later. A video may help creating the first document: http://tinyurl.com/FirstLatexPgm. An excellent and through introduction in 2.5 hours is found in the CTAN short introduction: https://ctan.org/pkg/lshort-english.

4.4 Bibliograpahy

Researchers often write extensive documents, such as reviews or grants, with 100 or more citations organized in the bibliography or reference section. The organization of those references and documents becomes paramount in these circumstances and the same process can be used and practiced with smaller documents.(Duong, 2010) The free multi-platform utility Zotero helps you collect, organize, cite and share research articles. It can be installed as a stand-alone application and minimizes the workflow. Next to the URL in the web browser the Zotero button will appear after successful installation. Pressing this button will export the complete citation information to the Zotero database. In Zotero, you can right-click the library and EXPORT LIBRARY ... in the format "BibTeX" to a file called "myBibtex.bib" in this example that can be directly included in a LaTeX document, see Listing 4.2. In addition to the filename, you also need to specify a style for the bibliography. The style can be customized, if needed. In the example of Listing 4.2 the style "plain" is used. The \nocite command makes sure that all citations in the included file are listed.

Listing 4.2: Example LaTeXcode on how to include a bibliography. A separate file called myBibtex.bib must exist. The extension is not included.

```
\documentclass{article}
\bibliographystyle{plain}
\begin{document}
\nocite{*}
\bibliography{myBibtex}
\end{document}
```

Depending on the compiler that you are using (TeXShop on Mac, WinShell on Windows), you may have to do a separate compilation for the BibTeX file, and compile the LaTeX file twice.

The location of the citation in the document is important. It appears at the end of the sentence or after the quotation, text that is borrowed from the cited document. The command \cite will place the proper citation in place.

An additional feature is implemented by installing the "Better Bib-TeX" add-on (https://zotplus.github.io/zotero-better-bibtex/) in Zotero. It will auto-sync a library, so that constant exporting is not needed. Secondly, selecting a reference in Zotero and using the copy command will generate the proper \cite command.

4.4.1 Zotero Activity

In this activity, you will learn how to cite articles. You will get familiar with the reference program Zotero (https://www.zotero.org/), and learn how to format references in different styles using BibTeX. You will also learn about how to search for articles using Web of Science. Your final work should list at least 5 review articles.

In the first part, start the application. Zotero is a program that is available on multiple platforms and allows you to collect, organize and cite research articles and resources easily. It will be particularly helpful, once you write longer articles, thesis, or dissertation.

1. Determine the *research topic* for the search

2. Start the program Zotero. If it is not installed, then install it from the website: `https://www.zotero.org/` (use Chrome browser and add the Zotero extension).

3. In Zotero, click on the MY LIBRARY folder and create a NEW COLLECTION named after your *research topic*.

Follow this example to find research articles on your topic.

1. Go to the Library page, and click on DATABASES BY TOPIC, then select "Physics & Astronomy".

2. You can choose any option, but for the purpose of this tutorial, we will continue using the "Web of Science" (WoS) database. If you access the database outside CSULB, you will need to use your studentID and password to use the service.

3. Choose ADVANCED SEARCH

4. Use the field tags to make a search, such as TS=YOURTOPIC AND TI=REVIEW, where you replace YOURTOPIC and then sort by citations. To first order, the most cited articles are important to the field, if the search returns a large number of articles.Try out different search strings to find good review articles on the topic of Nuclear Magnetic Resonance.

5. Choose an article and make sure that the abstract is interesting and really is a review paper on the topic. Tweak the search, if needed.

6. Click on the PAGE ICON next to the STAR ICON, see Fig 4.1.

7. Repeat process and add more references to your Zotero database.

8. You may also add a book on the topic.

Now returning to Zotero, right-click on your collection and click on EXPORT COLLECTION, see Fig. 4.1 c). The data is saved in a file that

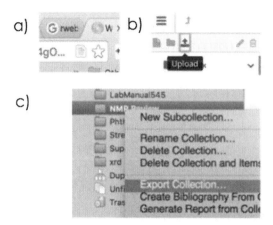

Figure 4.1: The Zotero reference managers allows you to quickly capture references from a) the browser by simply clicking on the book-shaped icon next to the star bookmarking icon. b) ShareLatex has an upload feature to add the bibliography file that you (c) export from Zotero in BıвТ_EX format. It is useful to sometimes save in "Western" format.

supports BıвТ_EX. It should have the ending .bib. Remove any spaces, underscores, and other strange symbols from the filename, as this could spell trouble later.

Now that the data has been exported, use a browser and open a new project in ShareLatex.

1. Go to `https://www.sharelatex.com/`

2. Login to your account (or make a free account, if needed).

3. Click on NEW PROJECT (blank project) and call it *research topic* or similar.

4. Hit the Upload button, see Fig. 4.1 b), and upload the BıвТ_EX file

5. Before `\begin{document}` write `\bibliographystyle{plain}`...

6. Before `\end{document}` write `\bibliography{Topic.bib}` (Note .bib extension is not necessary, but can be added, no spaces are allowed inside curly brackets.

7. Make sure that the bib file has no spaces, if so, replace with dashes.

8. Include all members' name in the `\author` argument

9. Change the title, and add some text for explanation of the document. Use the command \nocite{*} somewhere, so that all references will be added.

10. Add at least one citation directly, using the command \cite{name}, the name of the citation is in the bib file after @article{

11. Change the style of the bibliography from "plain" to something different.

12. Explore what difference the command \citeA makes.

13. Download and save PDF document.

4.5 Report Structure

Each journal requires a specific style and report structure that includes font size, graph quality, figure numeration, etc. The website for the journal denotes weather articles can be submitted in both Word format and/or in LaTeX format. LaTeX(note that the last letter is a Greek χ and not to be confused with the Latin letter "x") is a popular format for articles and books. It is not a WSYWYG (what you see is what you get) format like Word, but rather needs to be compiled into PDF or postscript format before it is distributed. The LaTeX format is very flexible, since the compiler takes care of table of contents, page numeration, page spacing and style.

For example, there is a LaTeX template to write a CSULB M.S. Thesis, see the resource page on the physics home page (http://www.csulb.edu/depts/physics/resources/thesis_resources.htm). Once you insert the text, it will compile and produce a document that complies with the specific CSULB library standards. It will also generate a table of content and list of figures and tables.

A scientific paper, M.S. thesis, or Ph.D. thesis is generally divided into 7 parts, each part will be explained in detail in the following:

- Header
- Introduction
- Experiment
- Results and Analysis
- Conclusion
- Acknowledgments

- Bibliography

Header The header includes a title, authors, author affiliations and an abstract. The title needs to be informative and necessarily reflect the goal of the experiment, but rather the result. The abstract contains all the information and main results and important conclusions of the paper. It is a quick way for a reader to get an idea of whether the article is of interest. A typical abstract has around 100 words and it is always a single paragraph.

Introduction The introduction provides sufficient background information and motivation to draw the reader in. Generally, this part will convince the reader that this particular research is worthwhile. Often conflicting models are described, advantages to certain techniques discussed, and the rationale for this experiment discussed. Only background information pertinent to the experiment should be provided.

Experiment The experiment describes the materials and method used. It should include the assumptions and background information of how samples were prepared, etc. The methodology is described, such that a reader would have sufficient information to duplicate the experiment and find the same results.

Results and Analysis The most important section contains the results of the experiment and their analysis. This section should include the necessary figures, graphs, and tables with captions to support the findings. The data of the graphs should be described and the implications discussed. Often, the results are compared to other similar research.

Conclusion This last short section summarizes the work and focuses the readers on the important findings without going into the details. It may reflect on special implications.

Acknowledgments This section acknowledges the funding sources, help with measurements and extra support from people who are not authors. This could refer to preparation of special substrates, the help with a particular measurements, or insightful discussions of the results and analysis with a peer.

Bibliography Previous research results should be cited throughout the text (except abstract) with the references listed here. Typical 3-

5 page papers have 10-30 references, whereas M.S. thesis have 25-50 references and Ph.D. theses usually have over 100 references. The bibliography contains authors, journal name, journal volume, issue number, page number, and year of publication at the minimum. Sometimes, it also includes the title of the paper. Websites are not good resources for citations, as they tend to change, get modified or deleted. Whenever possible, reference to scientific literature should be made.

Other important restrictions include adherence to page limits, proper numbering schemes of pages, tables, and figures, page limits, and proper formatting of graphs. Each table and each figure requires a caption explaining the main parts of the table or graph.

4.6 Units

In physics, the units of choice are based on the Système International (SI) units. Other common unit systems are the cgs system, which is based on centimeters, grams, and seconds; it is particularly popular in magnetism. Reports should exclusively use SI units with a few exceptions, which are for temperature, where degrees Celsius (°C) are also used. Note that the units are not spelled out, as in the following sample sentence: "The measured time constant $\tau = 52 \pm 3$ s". You would not write out the word "seconds". In LATEX, units are easily integrated in the package *siunitx*, which is loaded with the code in Listing 4.3. The command \SI uses two inputs, the number, and the units; you can use engineering notation for the number as shown in the example.

Listing 4.3: Code for displaying units properly can be done with the package *siunitx*. It will produce the proper spacings after the number and also write the units properly. In this case it will write 4.2×10^{-6} μm.

```
\usepackage{siunitx}
\begin{documentclass}
\SI{4e-6}{\meter}
\SI{4.2e-6}{\micro\meter}
\end{documentclass}
```

4.7 Presentations

Communication is a skill necessary in science. Research becomes the good of everyone; therefore dissemination is an important step of the research process. A presentation reaches a particular audience. The presentation should convey a particular message. This message is presented in the form of a logical story. There is a particular flow to this story.

The first slide is the title page, of course. It contains the carefully selected title, which should reveal the core of the message that you are going to present. It also has your name, your mentor's name, and other contributors. Equally important the funding source is also listed.

All slides should use a font size that can easily be read by the audience. A minimum font size of 24 is recommended. The type of font is also important. In print, a serif font is commonly used, but for slide presentations, the font ought to be sans-serif, such as Arial. Finally, the color contrast must be good.

The second slide is very important; it needs to capture the audience and explain why they must be interested in your story. This slide includes the motivation for the research and makes a compelling case. It should provide enough context to make the specific research necessary. Starting with a broad point of view that includes all audience members. The broad picture is quickly focused towards the topic of interest. A relatively simple way to improve the motivation part is to notice that the first paragraph of most journal articles, but in particular PRL articles, are dedicated to integrating the larger picture.

The following slides tell the logical story, so throw out parts that do not belong into that story. Slides should mostly include images, photos, and diagrams that complement the speaking portion. The slides should stay up sufficiently long. Do not include details on the slides that you will not discuss. Do not go back to previous slides. Avoid full sentences and text on slides as they lend to reading the slides. If necessary, repeat the slide in the deck, however, form the story so that it logically progresses and presents evidence supporting the message that you want to convey. The title of the slide - if there is a title at all - should express the message not the content; i.e. it should not be *results*, rather *spin-lattice relaxation*.

Good advice is to only include material on the slides that you are going to cover and to avoid using the whiteboard, or moving backwards in slides. That is where practice of your slides and your story comes in. Provide an accurate representation of your work and the work of others; i.e. only include graphs, photos, or diagrams that are not copyright protected and include a clear reference at the bottom of the page. It is a common practice to have a summary or conclusion as the last slide. The special vocabulary required in your talk needs to be explained carefully and used consistently.

Graphs should have clear labels and units and they must be pointed out in the talk. Data tables are not effective.

Finally, it help to give the presentation in professional attire and to speak clearly and hold a laser pointer firmly (two hands). Avoid making jokes and side remarks as those should only be given by the most practiced speakers.

4.8 Standard Operating Procedure

The standard operating procedure (SOP) is a step-by-step instruction set that includes important safety information. The SOP has a distinct style, quite different from the lab report. It should be succinct and very concise, all prosaic words need to be avoided. It allows someone to safely operate a tool. For instance, there is an SOP to operate each particular model of atomic force microscope. The document often includes bullet points. For the purpose of the advanced experimental laboratory, the SOP includes a few important sections, which are detailed below.

The title page should include the equipment model and version, also the physical location, date, authors and space for signature. This is part one. Each document is also versioned, so that it can be updated at a later moment. The second page, and second part, is a table of contents that lists the procedures that are discussed. In the third part, all procedures are listed. A procedure is a particular task, such as setting up the device, shut-down of the device or a particular measurement. It may include bullet points, graphical flowcharts, and hierarchal lists. A procedure starts with the scope and limitations. After the procedural section, in part 4 and 5, the checklist and trouble-shooting sections are added. The checklist is used to verify that the equipment is working properly, if there is an issue with the operation. The trouble-shooting section includes advice for common errors. Finally, the safety protocol is an important sixth chapter in the SOP.

Any good SOP includes diagrams, photos, and sketches. It should define acronyms and define terminology and abbreviations. The pages should be numbered, the document is dated. The document may include instructions on how to save files, extract data and how to convert files into standard file formats.

The grading rubric for the SOP is based on the following criteria:

1. Does it have a title page? Is the title clear and includes the model? Does the SOP include all parts?

2. Is the first page signed by all members?

3. Does the SOP have all 6 sections?

4. Is the language concise? And clear? And unambiguous?

5. Does it have diagrams, pictures, images, or schematics (DPIS)?

6. Are the DPIS clear and useful?

7. Do all DPIS have captions and are they copyright-free?

8. Are there steps missing in the procedure? Are the steps clear?

9. Are the pages numbered? Is the footer correct?

10. Are exact part numbers for the equipment, preparation method listed?

11. Are the references properly formatted?

12. Is the SOP complete?

13. Can an operator execute the procedures without further documentation?

14. Overall impression

4.9 Data Analysis and Graphs

Modern data sets are large, so software must be used for analysis. Open-source software tools are particularly enticing. While plotting software, such as GnuPlot provide flexibility in making modern graphs, a more comprehensive plotting software is Python or the R Project, which run on many platforms. The R project can be used for batch data analysis, data fitting, modeling, and graphing. The language is most similar to MatLab and has many packages that extend its functionality. To follow this tutorial, you will need to install the R environment (`https://www.r-project.org/`) and RStudio (`https://www.rstudio.com/`), which provides an open-source graphical interface for R. Alternatively, it is possible to run R in the cloud at R-Fiddle (`http://www.r-fiddle.org/#/`).

In R language, data is processed in so-called data frames. A data frame is similar to a table and contains many labeled columns, which have data stored in rows. A data column is generated from a vector using the command `c()`. As an example, we will make a plot of the average temperatures of Long Beach.This data frame has 3 columns, called month, TL and TH. Note that the colon makes a sequence of numbers from 1 to 12 and stores it as a vector.

```
T.high = c(20,20,20,22,23,25,28,29,28,25,22,19)
T.low = c(8,9,10,12,14,16,18,18,17,15,10,8)
month = 1:12
data = data.frame(month=month, TL = T.low, TH = T.high )
```

Here is the code to make a plot using the package `ggplot`, which you can install with the command `install.packages('ggplot2')`. Additionally, we are calculating the medium temperature by adding a new column to the data frame called `Tm`. The aesthetics in ggplot defines the x and y variables of the plot, which are `month` and `Tm`. Since the label of the y-axis requires a superscript, an expression is used. The last part chooses the number of breaks along the x-axis, in this case 6.

```
library(ggplot2)
data$Tm = (data$TH+data$TL)/2
exp.Temp = expression(paste('T ('^o,'C)'))
ggplot(data, aes(month, Tm, ymax=TH, ymin=TL)) +
  geom_point(size=3, color='blue') +
  geom_errorbar(color='blue') +
  theme_bw() + ylab(exp.Temp) +
  scale_x_continuous(breaks = seq(2, 12, 2))
```

The resulting plot is shown in Fig. 4.2. It can be saved with the command `ggsave('graph.png')` in R.

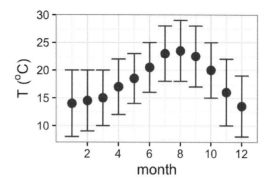

Figure 4.2: Average high and low monthly temperatures in Long Beach, CA as plotted in R.

The following example (graph shown in Fig. 4.3) demonstrates making a quick graph from data collected on the Rigaku Smartlab x-ray diffractometer. The diffractometer saves files in the RAS format, which can be opened with a text editor. The data is read from the RAW file with the command **read.csv**. The header lines are automatically ignored as they start with a comment symbol. The third column **V3** is deleted, as it is not needed here. Next, the columns for data frame **d** are relabeled with **names**. In order to express Greek symbols in the x-axis, the command **expression** is used. It also allows to include superscripts with the symbol ^ and subscripts by enclosing the subscript in square brackets ([0]).

```
fname = '~/RAW/Ld20160514.ras'
d <- read.csv(fname, header=FALSE, comment.char= "*",sep=" ")
d$V3 <- NULL
names(d) = c('TwoTheta','I')
exp.TwoTheta=expression(paste('2',theta,' ('^o,')'))
ggplot(d, aes(TwoTheta, I)) +
  geom_line(col='red') + theme_bw() +
  scale_x_continuous(limits=c(5,30)) + scale_y_log10() +
  xlab(exp.TwoTheta) + ylab('I (a.u.)')
```

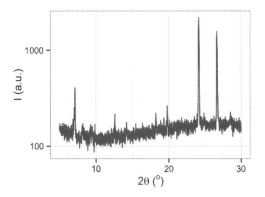

Figure 4.3: The following is the result of the code on page 36 loading and displaying x-ray data. The spectrum shows the Bragg-Brentano scattering from iron phthalocyanine powder.

4.10 Fitting of Data

The prevalent theme in physics is to make predictions based on a model. The experiment allows us either to confirm the predictions through strategic measurements, or to modify and extend a model. In this process, data is collected, graphed, and then compared with the model. Ideally, the model would quantitatively predict the experimental data. In practice, however, there may be some adjustable parameters that need to be fit. Therefore, fitting data is a common and useful practice.

A simple way to fit data is to linearize the experimental data, so that the fitting parameters are either the slope or the offset of a linear equation. A transformation of variables is done, so that the transformed equation has the shape of $y(x) = A + Bx$, where B is the slope and A is the offset. By plotting the data in the transformed variables, a ruler can be used to determine the fit parameters A and B. Alternatively, a program is used to help you fit the data, generally using a non-linear least square fit. In R language, the function lm is used to get a least-square linear fit.

As a practical example, if your data has the form of an exponential decay, such as in $M(t) = M_0 \exp(-t/T_1)$, then linearization would occur in the following way:

$$\ln\frac{M(t)}{M_0} = -\frac{1}{T_1}t$$

we have introduced a new variable $y \equiv \ln M(t)/M_0$ and the running variable $x \equiv t$ is the time. The offset would represent the amplitude of the exponential decay $A = \ln M_0$, and the slope of the linear equation is equal to $B = -(1/T_1)$ in this representation.

The following example provides code to make a fit using R. In the first part, the data is loaded from a file generated by the Tektronix oscilloscope, which is in a comma-separated format. The command to load the data into a data frame is called read.csv.

```
# Loading data from Tektronix oscilloscope
data <- read.csv('20160303-BDBL-NMR-FID1.csv', header=FALSE)
names(data)[4:5] = c('time','V')      # label columns
data$time = data$time*1E3             # convert s to ms
q = subset(data, time < -0.1)         # correct for offset
data$V = data$V - mean(q$V)
```

This data frame contains two columns labeled time and V, which contains the time in units of ms and the electric potential measured in units of V. A graph is generated by first invoking plot to generate the data points. A second layer is added with the command points in order to highlight the data points that will be used for the fit.

```
plot(data$time, data$V, xlab='time(ms)', ylab=('V(V)'),
     ylim=c(-0.2, 1.3), xlim=c(-0.5, 3))
d <- subset(data, time>0.3)           # fit subset of data
points(d$time, d$V, col='red')
```

R provides a straight-forward way to make a non-linear fit to the data using the command nls, which takes 3 main parameters. The first parameter is the data frame that contains the data to be fit. Next the model is described, which is $V = A\exp[-time/T]$, where A and T are fitting parameters, and the others are variables defined in the data frame. The fit will only work, if reasonable starting fit parameters are provided. The starting parameters are provided in the form of a list. The result of the fit is stored in a variable called fit.

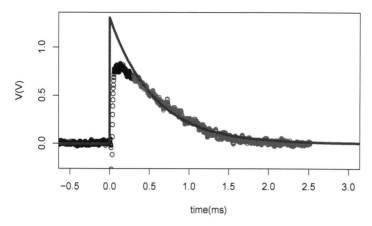

Figure 4.4: Measurement of a free induction decay from protons in glycerin. The graph is generated with R, where data points (circle) represent voltage measured after a $90°$ pulse was applied to create precession. The relaxation of the signal amplitude is modeled and fit with an exponential decay (see text on page 38).

The fit line is added to the plot by using **predict** to compute values along some time values. In this case a vector with 100 elements is generated, the time running from 0 to two times the maximum. The fit is overlaid using blue color and line thickness of 4. The result of this code is shown in Fig. 4.4.

```
# do fitting, giving some reasonable starting values
nls(data = d, V ~ A*exp(-time/T), start=list(A=1, T=1)) -> fit
time.fit = seq(from =0, to =max(d$time)*2, length.out=100)
predict(fit, list(time=time.fit))->V.fit
time.fit=c(-1,0,time.fit)
V.fit = c(0,0, V.fit)
lines(time.fit, V.fit, col='blue', lwd=4)
```

It is noteworthy that **plot** will clear the graph, but you can still add data later using either **lines** or **points** for adding data with a line or data points, respectively. The fitting parameters can be separately listed with **summary(fit)$coeff**.

The same plot can also be graphed with the previously mentioned **ggplot2** package. A common way to use **ggplot** is to make a table with three columns (using **melt** package for complex data). The first column is the x-axis, the second the y-axis, and the third column defines the data set for which automatically a legend is displayed. In the following example, the NMR FID data is appended to the fitting data, by using the row binding function `rbind`. The third column is called `label` and is filled with the label for each row. The command `length` returns the number of items in a vector and `nrow` returns the number of rows of a data frame. Finally, the axes are labeled and the title of the legend, which would be "label", is hidden. The `legend.key` element defines the square around each of the items in the legend.

```
myData = data.frame(time = time.fit, V = V.fit)
myData = rbind(myData, cbind(time = data$time, V = data$V))
myData$label = c(rep('fit',length(time.fit)),
                 rep('data', nrow(data)))
ggplot(myData, aes(time, V, color=label, linetype= label))+
  geom_line(size=2) + theme_bw(base_size=22) +
  xlab('time (s)') + ylab('V (V)') +
  scale_y_continuous(limits=c(-0.2,1.4)) +
  scale_x_continuous(limits=c(-0.8, 2.6),
                     breaks=seq(-0.5,2.5,0.5)) +
  theme(legend.position = c(0.1, 0.9),
        legend.title = element_text(color=NA),
        legend.key = element_rect(colour = NA))
```

Problem 1 - Find a citation for a review article on the topic of *"nuclear magnetic resonance"* or *"atomic force microscopy"*.

Problem 2 - Find the h-factor of a famous physicist or a physicist in your department.

Problem 3 - Find the impact factor for the most recent years of two journals listed on page 21.

Problem 4 - Use the procedure listed on page 22 to find the main motivation for scientists studying *"superconductivity"* in recent years.

Problem 5 - Download the monthly average temperature of your city of choice and fit the temperature data to a sinusoidal function using a two-parameter fit that includes the amplitude and phase shift. Graph the results.

5 Nuclear Magnetic Resonance

MANY modern applications in physics, chemistry, biology, engineering, and medicine are based on the nuclear magnetic resonance (NMR) technique. This part will familiarize you with the pulsed nuclear magnetic resonance (PNMR) method and its many applications. Related techniques include magnetic resonance imaging (MRI) and electron paramagnetic resonance (EPR), also known as electron spin resonance (ESR). We will use the 15 MHz PNMR setup, which allows for measurements of the free induction decay (FID) in glycerine and other proton-rich materials.

5.1 Nuclear Spin

Nuclear magnetic resonance spectra can be used to learn about how complex molecules are organized. The molecule is put in a constant magnetic field. Then, the magnetic pulse perturbs the system, such that nuclear spins (protons, neutrons) are excited and resonate between discrete energy levels. The emitted signal, free induction decay (FID), can be picked up by coils and interpreted. The FID signal contains information about the chemistry of the atomic arrangement in the molecule. In magnetic resonance imaging (MRI), the signal contains information about the density of nuclear spins in space.

The discovery of nuclear magnetic resonance (NMR) received several Nobel prizes, see Table 5.1. The phenomenon concerns the nucleus of an atom. Fundamentally, a magnetic field is produced by a moving charge. In an atom, the electron has a spin and orbital momentum, but the nucleus (proton, neutron) also has a spin (nuclear spin). All spins have quantized energies in multiples of $\hbar$. These quanta are generally expressed in S, L (angular momentum quantum number), and I. The nucleus can have a spin (nuclear spin), which is generally denoted by I. A free proton or neutron has a nuclear spin $I = \frac{1}{2}$. A non-zero nuclear spin is observed if the proton number is even and, or the neutron number is even.

Notably, the spin of the electron cannot be probed classically as pointed out by Bohr (1925). It is a quantum-mechanical phenomenon. Namely, in 1925, Pauli published a seminal paper on the exclusion principle and declared that some nuclei should also possess an angular momentum (Pauli, 1925). Earlier, the experimental results from Paschen showed spectral lines that were not expected, but if one understood, as Goudsmit (student of Ehrenfest) and Uhlenbeck did, that the electron carries both an angular momentum and an intrinsic spin with their associated quantum numbers m_l and m_s, then the spectrum could be explained. The electron spin, then, could also explain some *complicated* Zeeman effects and everything fell into place. The neutron in the nucleus had, of course, not been discovered yet. In 1932, Chadwick, student of Rutherford, published *possible existence of a neutron* in Nature. While it was first clear that the electron had an intrinsic spin, it became understood that the proton and the neutron would also contain spin. While the electron's angular momentum can be conceptualized classically (orbital motion), the nuclear's spin cannot be perceived as such, as it is purely a quantum mechanical phenomenon. Even though protons have a complicated structure based on quarks and gluons, the spin is rather simple, just one half. It is estimated that about half of the proton's spin originates from the gluons, while about a third comes from the three quarks, leaving some unknowns.

On the experimental side, Rabi took on the task to find the nuclear spin of sodium. His character was such that he wanted to design a simple, clean, and clever experiment to measure it. So, in 1937 Rabi predicted that by tuning a radio-frequency excitation signal to the Larmor frequency, the absorbed energy could flip the spin orientation. A year later, his team succeeded in observing the magnetic resonance phenomenon that was specific or characteristic to each atom or molecule. While this work was focused on atoms, Purcell (Harvard) and Bloch (Stanford) extended the method to liquids and solids a few years later. Hahn observed that there is a spin echo in 1949 (Hahn, 1950). This experiment will be performed in Sec. 9.5. At the same time, chemical shifts were observed due to the local changes in magnetic fields from electron cloud shielding in molecules. In the medical field, NMR was first used in 1977 to generate a two-dimensional image of the proton density of soft tissues, what is now known as medical resonance imaging

Year	Person	Title
1943	Otto Stern	development of molecular ray method and his discovery of the magnetic moment of the proton
1944	Isidor Isaac Rabi	resonance method for recording the magnetic properties of atomic nuclei
1952	Felix Bloch Edward Purcell	development of new methods for nuclear magnetic precision measurements
1991	Richard Ernst	method of high-resolution NMR spectroscopy
2002	Kurt Wüthrich	using NMR for determining the three-dimensional structure of biological macromolecules

Table 5.1: Selected Nobel prizes in physics for NMR. The last two prizes were given in the field of chemistry.

(MRI), see page 54. This technique relies on Fourier transformations, which became more feasible with the growth in computational technologies. While NMR was initially developed in physics, it spread quickly into chemistry, bio-chemistry and medicine.

Let us start on some common ground with basic background information. For an electron on a classical orbit, the magnetic moment is defined by its current density $\vec{j}$:

$$\vec{\mu} \equiv \frac{1}{2} \int \vec{r} \times \vec{j} \; d^3r, \tag{5.1}$$

which can be rewritten - for the purpose of clarity here - for a uniform current density with the current I and the cross-sectional area A of a wire. It then follows that for a single electron that the magnetic moment is expressed as

$$\mu = IA = \frac{e}{T}\pi R^2, \tag{5.2}$$

where T is the *classical* time that the electron takes to orbit the nucleus once. This time can be expressed as $T = \frac{2\pi R}{v}$, such that orbital magnetic moment of the electron is

$$\mu = \frac{e}{2}vR = \frac{e}{2m_e}L. \tag{5.3}$$

The classical angular momentum L is the product of $m_e R v$. Quantum-mechanically, L is quantized, where $L = N\hbar$ and N is an integer. It is then natural to define the smallest magnetic moment - called Bohr magneton - which is given by

$$\mu_B = \frac{e\hbar}{2m_e},$$

(5.4)

where e is the charge of the electron and m_e the mass of the electron. Since the proton is massively heavier, a magnetic moment from its spin is smaller by the same fraction.

Now, we can define the magnetic moment quite generally as:

$$\mu = g_I \frac{e\hbar}{2m_{e,p}} m_I$$

(5.5)

where g_I is the gyromagnetic factor, $m_{e,p}$ is the mass of the electron or proton respectively, and $m_{S,L,I}$ are the quantum numbers for electron spin, electron angular momentum and nuclear spin. For a proton m_I has only two values, a $\pm 1/2$.

It follows that due to the mass of the proton and neutron compared to the electron's mass, the magnetic moment is about $2000\times$ smaller for nuclei. Therefore, electronic properties can largely ignore the nuclear spins.

The gyromagnetic factor takes into account the geometry of the particle. The value of g is $g_S \simeq -2$, $g_L = -1$, and $g_I = 5.58$ for a proton and $g_I = -3.82$ for a neutron. The discrepancy of the $g_{I,p}/g_{I,n}$ ratio from $3/2$ is due to the color charge of quarks explained in quantum chromodynamics.

The potential energy U of an atom with the nucleus spin aligned and anti-aligned to an external magnetic field $\vec{B}$ is given by the following dot product.

$$U = -\vec{\mu} \cdot \vec{B}$$

(5.6)

The energy difference for the hydrogen atom with $I=2$ which has only two states (between $m_I = +1/2$ and $m_I = -1/2$) in a magnetic field along the z-direction B_z is

$$\Delta E = g_I \frac{e\hbar}{2m_p} B_z = \gamma \hbar B_z.$$

(5.7)

isotope	spin I	magnetic moment μ/μ_N	magnetogyric ratio γ 10^7 rad/Ts	NMR frequency MHz
electron	0.5	-3184.0	-17610	65820.0
neutron	0.5	-3.3	-18	68.5
hydrogen	0.5	4.8	27	100.0
^{13}C	0.5	1.2	7	25.1
^{19}F	0.5	4.6	25	94.1
^{23}Na	1.5	2.9	7	26.5
^{113}Cd	0.5	-1.1	-6	22.2
^{195}Pt	0.5	1.0	6	21.4

Table 5.2: Nuclear spin properties according to R.K. Harris.(Harris, 1986) NMR frequencies given for B=2.35 T.

Here, the material specific property γ is called the gyromagnetic ratio and defined as,

$$\gamma \equiv g_I \frac{e}{2m_p} \tag{5.8}$$

Typical values for γ are listed in Tab. 5.2. The units of γ are energy per Tesla per Planck's constant $\hbar$. The energy gap ΔE is directly proportional to the applied magnetic field with γ as the slope. The gap can be increased by increasing the magnetic field or using nuclei with large γ values.

In an external magnetic field $\vec{B}$ the magnetic moment of the nuclear spin will precess with an angular frequency ν, called the Larmor frequency. The precession is similar to the mechanical precession of a bicycle tire due to the force from the Earth, see Fig. 5.1.

How fast does it precess? That depends on the energy difference between the two energy levels, specifically $\Delta E = \hbar\omega = h\nu$, where ν is the Larmor frequency. Since typical laboratory magnetic fields are in the range of 0.5 to 10 T, it follows that typical frequencies are on the order of 10 – 1000 MHz, the radio frequency range of electro-magnetic waves. For a magnetic field of 2.35 T, a proton would resonate at 100 MHz.

From a quantum mechanical approach, even a single proton is in a superposition state of spin-up and spin-down. The probability of finding the proton in the up or down state is given by the Boltzmann factor, see Eq. 5.13. Either of those two states are difficult to measure.

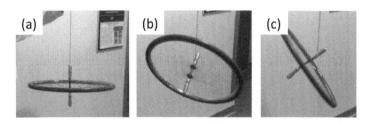

Figure 5.1: In the classical analog of precession, a spinning bicycle wheel experiences the force of the Earth's magnetic field. (a) The precession cannot be measured when the spin axis is aligned with the Earth's field. A torque is exerted onto the wheel, so that it precesses at an angle. At different moments in time, it will be in position (b) and (c). The period to finish one rotation is a characteristic time.

In the mechanical analogue shown in Fig. 5.1, it corresponds to the first figure, when the Earth's gravitational force is aligned with the angular momentum of the wheel. It is necessary to tilt the magnetic spin away from the magnetic field $\vec{B_0}$ in a direction normal to the z-axis. There, the nuclear spin can precess and the time-changing moment induces a current through Faraday induction in a receiving coil.

In the depicted example of Fig. 5.1, the bicycle while is spinning rapidly. In equilibrium the wheel's spin direction is aligned with the Earth's gravitational field. It is possible - by applying a manual force - to torque the wheel into precession. The wheel's precession is now clearly visible.

How can the spin direction be changed? A secondary coil may create a magnetic field to tip the spins over by the torque that it creates. The same coil maybe used to pick-up the signal. First, a pulse is emitted to create a magnetic field perpendicular to the z-axis (direction of $\vec{B_0}$), after the pulse the induced current is measured as a function of time. This pulse is called a 90° pulse corresponding to a pulse that lasts for one forth of a full precession rotation.

5.2 Larmor Precession

As mentioned, the nucleus, both a proton and a neutron, have a magnetic moment $\vec{\mu}$, a pseudovector. The magnetic moment can be split into two components, one part is given by the geometry and the second part can be controlled and is related to the spin. Combining Eqs. 5.5 and 5.8, the magnetic moment of a nucleus is the written as

$$\vec{\mu} = \gamma \vec{I}, \qquad (5.9)$$

where γ is the gyromagnetic ratio and the $\vec{I}$ is the angular momentum vector, which is quantized. Assuming that the angular momentum is along the z-axis, for example, we can write the quantization for the angular momentum as follows: $I_z = m\hbar$, where m is a half-integer. For example, for $I_z = 1/2$, it follows that m can assume two values, namely $\pm 1/2$.

As mentioned in Sec. 5.3, it would be difficult to control a single nucleus, therefore experiments are usually setup for a collection of spins. A constant magnetic field $\vec{B}_0$ is used to polarize the nuclei in a particular direction. On average, at finite temperature, not all spins will point into this direction, but a majority - determined classically by Boltzmann-Maxwell distribution - will orient themselves in that direction. Applying a secondary RF magnetic field perpendicular to the DC polarizing magnetic field would give the nuclei a "kick" to precess. This precession happens at a frequency referred to as the Larmor frequency.

Let us first realize that the magnetic moment of the nucleus $\vec{\mu}$ experiences a force in the presence of a magnetic field $\vec{B}$. Then, there will be a torque

$$\tau = \mu B \sin \theta = \gamma I B \sin \theta \qquad (5.10)$$

where θ is the angle between the magnetic field and the direction of the spin. The precession means the protection of the angular momentum $(I \sin \theta)$ is changing with time, namely that $\Delta I = I \sin \theta \Delta \phi$, so that we can write using the conservation of angular momentum $\vec{\tau} = d\vec{I}/dt$,

$$\gamma I B \sin \theta = \frac{I \sin \theta d\phi}{dt} \qquad (5.11)$$

so that we can determine the precession angular frequency ω, which is called the Larmor frequency

$$\omega_{Larmor} = \frac{d\phi}{dt} = \gamma B \qquad (5.12)$$

Using this relation, we find that for a magnetic field of 1 T, the Larmor frequency for a proton would be 42.6 MHz. The tuning of the PNMR oscillator to the Larmor resonance frequency will be a very accurate reading of the magnetic field $\vec{B}$, when the gyromagnetic ratio is known with high precision.

5.3 Boltzmann statistics

For a macroscopic system that is in thermal equilibrium at temperature T, the probability $P(E_i)$ of finding particles in a discrete energy state E_i is given by the Boltzmann factor, which is the exponent in the following equation.

$$P(E_i) = \frac{1}{Z} \exp\left(-\frac{E_i}{k_B T}\right) \tag{5.13}$$

Here $1/Z$ is a normalization factor, where Z is commonly called the partition function (Zustandssumme). For a system with only two states $P_{+1/2}$ and $P_{-1/2}$, $Z = \exp(-\frac{E_+}{kT}) + \exp(-\frac{E_-}{kT})$. The condition to find the spin in one state is written as $P(E_-) + P(E_+) = 1$. At finite temperatures, the majority of spins will be randomly pointing up and down, even in the presence of a relatively strong magnetic field. Only the spin difference ΔN is relevant for the net polarization and it can be calculated as $\Delta N = N_+ - N_-$, where $N_+ = P_{+1/2} N$.

From one of the exercises, we find that the difference in number of nuclei with spin-up and spin-down is given by,

$$\Delta N = N \frac{\Delta E}{2 k_B T}, \tag{5.14}$$

where N is the total number of atoms. The number of active nuclei, or signal strength, can be increased by going to lower temperature, by increasing the volume of material (N), or by increasing the energy gap (more magnetic field or high gyromagnetic moment of nucleus).

Let P be the probability per unit time and per spin of a transition induced by a perturbation through a perpendicular magnetic field B_1. Then, we can find the rate of transitions, which is $R = P\Delta E \Delta N$. The detector coils actually measure the induced current from a magnetic flux change $emf = -d\Phi/dt$, and therefore the observed signal S can be written as,(Harris, 1986)

$$S \sim \frac{\gamma^4 B_0^2 N B_1}{T} \tag{5.15}$$

48

We observe that there is a strong dependence on γ, refer to Tab. 5.2. Also, high constant magnetic fields B_0 are desirable to increase the signal. The signal strength is proportional to the sample size N. The signal can further be improved by lowering the temperature.

Importantly, the nucleus is somewhat shielded of the magnetic field B_0 by the surrounding electrons. This shielding reduces the effective magnetic field at the nucleus' location by a small fraction σ, so that the effective magnetic field can be written as

$$B_{eff} = B_0(1 - \sigma) \tag{5.16}$$

Since $\omega = \gamma B$, the Larmor frequency may vary for the same nuclei in a given molecule. The shielding leads to a chemical shift. This chemical shift is generally measured with reference to a standard as it is much easier to measure a difference rather than an absolute value. One common standard is tetramethylsilane, $Si(CH_3)_4$, or TMS. The shift is then expressed in terms of δ, where $\delta = 10^6(\sigma_{TMS} - \sigma_{sample})$.

The shielding constant σ is the sum of three contributions. The first contribution σ_{loc} is due to the electrons on the atom that contains the nucleus; the second part σ_{mol} is the contribution from the other parts of the molecule that further shield the magnetic field. Additionally, the third part is shielding from the solvent, which may be used.

The local contribution is the sum of a diamagnetic and paramagnetic signal. The Lamb equation provides a way to compute the diamagnetic contribution

$$\sigma_{loc,dia} = \frac{e^2 \mu}{3m_e} \int_0^\infty \rho(r)r \; dr \tag{5.17}$$

In hydrogen, ^{1}H, there is only 1 s-orbital, which implies that the diamagnetic contribution dominates and can be computed based on the electron density $\rho(r)$. The computations become quickly complex, so measured values of the shielding constant σ are often compared to known values using tables.

5.4 Bloch Equations

For many nuclei, we define the polarization as $\vec{M} = \sum \vec{\mu}_i$. In the presence of a magnetic field $\vec{B}$, the nuclear spins can precess around a constant magnetic field. This precession can be mathematically realized understanding the conservation of angular momentum,

$$\frac{d\vec{M}}{dt} = \gamma \left(\vec{M} \times \vec{B} \right) \tag{5.18}$$

Solving this equation, we find that the spin will process forever. The differential equations can be solved for the special case of $\vec{B}_0 =< 0, 0, B_0 >$,

$$\frac{dM_x}{dt} = -\gamma M_y B_z = \omega_0 M_y \tag{5.19}$$

$$\frac{dM_y}{dt} = -\gamma M_x B_z = \omega_0 M_x \tag{5.20}$$

$$\frac{dM_z}{dt} = 0 \tag{5.21}$$

Therefore, the z-component of the magnetization is constant; i.e. $M_z(t) = M_{0,z}$ and through substitution of $Q \equiv M_x + iM_y$, we find that the first two equations can be written as

$$\frac{d}{dt}Q = -i\omega_0 Q \tag{5.22}$$

with the solutions $M_x(t) = M_{0,x}\cos(\omega_0 t)$ and $M_y(t) = M_{0,y}\sin(\omega_0 t)$. Notably, the polarization along the x-axis will oscillate at the Larmor frequency and precess forever. In reality, this is not observed due to interactions of the nuclear spins with the environment. Swiss physicist Felix Bloch expressed this relaxation empirically by introduction of an additional term in the equations of motion, which can be expressed as a diagonal matrix $\vec{R}$,

$$\vec{R} = \begin{pmatrix} \frac{1}{T_2} & 0 & 0 \\ 0 & \frac{1}{T_2} & 0 \\ 0 & 0 & \frac{1}{T_1} \end{pmatrix} \tag{5.23}$$

and rewrote the Eq. 5.18 into a new equation, which is now known as the Bloch equation:

$$\frac{d\vec{M}}{dt} = \gamma \left(\vec{M} \times \vec{B} \right) - \vec{R} \left(\vec{M} - \vec{M}_0 \right) \tag{5.24}$$

where $\vec{M}_0$ is the equilibrium polarization, which can be written as

$$\vec{M}_0 = N\frac{\gamma^2 I(I+1)}{3k_B T}\vec{B}_0 \tag{5.25}$$

In the special case, that the magnetic field points along the z-axis, we then have the following three Bloch equations:

$$\frac{dM_x}{dt} = \gamma\left(M_y B_z - M_z B_y\right) - \frac{M_x}{T_2} \tag{5.26}$$

$$\frac{dM_y}{dt} = \gamma\left(M_z B_x - M_x B_z\right) - \frac{M_y}{T_2} \tag{5.27}$$

$$\frac{dM_z}{dt} = \gamma\left(M_x B_y - M_y B_x\right) - \frac{M_z}{T_1} + \frac{M_0}{T_1} \tag{5.28}$$

The two relaxation times that were introduced can be understood as the spin-lattice relaxation T_1 and the spin-spin relaxation T_2. These interactions decay exponentially with the characteristic times T_1 and T_2. We solve Bloch's equations with a constant magnetic field in the z-direction. The solutions are

$$M_x(t) = e^{-t/T_2}\left(M_{0,x}\cos(\omega_0 t) + M_{0,y}\sin(\omega_0 t)\right) \tag{5.29}$$

$$M_z(t) = M_0 + (M_{0,z} - M_0)e^{-t/T_1} \tag{5.30}$$

From these equations, you can see that the z-component relaxes with the time constant T_1, where as the x- and y- components are relaxing with a characteristic time of T_2. Both equations are graphed in Fig. 5.2.

5.5 Pulse Sequence

The principle of nuclear magnetic resonance (NMR) is the ability to excite nuclear spins with radio frequency pulses. When the nuclei revert back to equilibrium, they emit RF radiation that is detected. The signal contains the unique signature of the nuclear spin energy gap.

Given the Larmor frequency of a proton in the presence of a strong magnetic field, precession can occur if a pulse of accurate length is applied at the proper frequency to the sample. The resonance frequency is tuned by mixing the RF sample signal with a continuous wave (CW)

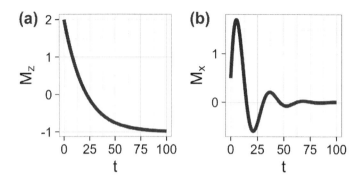

Figure 5.2: (a) Graph for $M_z(t)$ for $M_0 = -1$, $M_{0,z} = 2$, and $T_1 = 20$ with no units according to Eq. 5.30, and (b) graph for $M_x(t)$ using $\omega = 0.2$, and $M_{0,x} = 0.5$, $M_{0,y} = 2.5$.

RF signal. If the frequency from the sample is out of tune, a beating pattern will be observed. Changing the frequency allows the complete elimination of the beating and ensures that you are at resonance frequency. That frequency changes due to the change in temperature in the room, which affects the magnetization of the permanent magnet that polarizes the sample.

At resonance frequency, pulse sequences are used to probe the sample. The simplest pulse is a 90° pulse. Here, the angle corresponds to a particular time, which is related to the resonance frequency. Therefore, the 180° pulse is twice as long. In the mechanical analogue, consider a swing: the resonance frequency of the swing is given by the length of the strings and the mass of the Earth. Your friend asks you to swing them higher, increase the amplitude. First of all, your push needs to have the same frequency as the resonance frequency of the swing; it also needs to be in phase. Lastly, you can push for different amount of lengths. If you swing from the highest point, to the lowest point, it would correspond to a 90° *pulse.*

Using the pulse generator, the pulse is programmed and submitted as an RF pulse to the sample. The oscilloscope is triggered at the beginning of the pulse and subsequent pulses are spaced by the repetition time, which must be large enough to avoid overlap - take a moment to understand that. The precession is maximal at 90°, therefore the signal that is picked up, also called the free induction decay, will have a maximum at 90°. For a rotation of 180° there is no precession, the nuclear spin was simply reversed from the direction of the strong magnetic field and will decay back in sufficient time. However, 270° will again produce a maximum signal. Technically, there is a phase difference, however in the experimental setup, generally only the amplitude is plotted, therefore a 90° and 270° pulse will look alike. Still, you can distinguish the two pulses by continuously increasing the time and noting the number of the peak. The first maximum corresponds to a 90° peak, while the first minimum is a 180° degree pulse. This can be confirmed using the oscilloscope and explicit measurement of the time of each pulse.

The spin-lattice relaxation time T_1 is measured using a 180° - τ - 90° sequence, where the delay time τ is varied. For very small delay times ($\tau \ll T_1$), the free induction decay maximum voltage measured after the second pulse (90°) will have a value similar to measurements when the delay time is very long ($\tau \gg T_1$). At intermediate delay times the free induction decay signal vanishes. This happens essentially in the situation when you reverse the polarization of the nuclear spin with the 180° and wait long enough for the majority to relax half-way back to the equilibrium position to apply a 90° peak, the spins will not precess.

For the spin-spin relaxation time T_2, the measurement is opposite. Here the 90° - τ - 180° sequence is applied. In the so-called Carr and Purcell pulse sequence (Carr & Purcell, 1954), several consecutive 180° pulses are applied with the timing, such that the temporal space between 180° pulses is exactly twice the time τ from the 90° pulse to the first 180° pulse. Some time after the second pulse, namely τ, there is an echo, known as spin echo first detailed by Hahn (1950). The voltage amplitude of that echo relative to the original peak gives an estimate of how many spins have not yet lost phase. The amplitude of the spin echoes decreases exponentially with the time constant of T_2. The spin-spin relaxation time T_2 has to be smaller than the T_1 relaxation time.

Experimentally, the spin-spin relaxation measurements uses a long sequence of 180° pulses. If the pulse is not precisely 180°, then the error is propagated and after 10 – 30 pulses leads to significant errors. A solution to this problem was given by Meiboom and Gill (1958). They use the Carr and Purcell pulse sequence, but after the first pulse, a phase shift of 90° is introduced. This shift is relative to the original 90° pulse and with respect to the following 180° pulses. Secondly, successive pulses are coherent, which means that the direction of the RF pulses creating the small magnetic field is the same for all pulses.

5.6 Magnetic Resonance Imaging

The magnetic resonance image scanner allows a 3D view of the internal structure of the human body. It is based on nuclear magnetic resonance and adds spatial resolution to it. The spatial resolution is obtained through that fact that the resonance frequency changes with the magnitude of the applied magnetic field (refer to Eq. 5.7). If a magnetic field gradient is produced, the spatially varying magnetic field will produce a spectrum of frequencies. The intensities would vary depending on the number of spins with that particular resonance frequency. Using a Fourier analysis, it is possible to deconvolve this signal and produce a 2D spatial image, which if repeated can produce a 3D view into the sample or human body.

The time-varying magnetic fields, or microwaves, can heat the body just like a microwave. The precise calculation is involved, but a general rule of thumb is that a specific absorption rate (SAR) of $4\,W/kg$ causes the core temperature to rise by $1\,°C$(Freeman, 2003).

In the early 1970s, it became clear that NMR can be used to detect malignant tissue. In x-ray diffraction, the contrast scales with the square of the atomic number ($\sim Z^2$), so that high-density material (calcium in bones) can be easily analyzed. On the other hand, NMR can be tuned to the Larmor frequency of hydrogen and probe soft tissues, such as gray and white matter, muscles, fluids, and fat. The majority of the human body is composed of water and fat and other hydrogen containing atoms. The hydrogen nucleus has a very high gyromagnetic ratio, so that high sensitivity can be obtained. In addition to the general setup for NMR, magnetic resonance imaging (MRI) uses an additional gradient magnetic field.

The strong constant magnetic field polarizes the nuclei. At room temperature, far from all spins align with the magnetic field. Typically, about half the spins are aligned, and the other half are anti-aligned, and it is only the small excess of nuclei (about one in a million), which point in the direction of the magnetic field that contribute to the MRI signal. On top of this strong constant field, a magnetic field gradient is applied, so that the magnetic field at the top is slight different as opposed to at the bottom. A secondary magnetic field perpendicular to the first magnetic field, provides the 90° pulse for the nuclear spins to start precession. The spin-lattice relaxation ensures that the precession will vanish after the characteristic time T_1, which is 500 ms to 900 ms for brain matter. During this relaxation time, RF radiation corresponding to the Larmor frequency is emitted and detected with an RF coil.

The detected RF signal would be composed of a single frequency, if the Larmor frequency were the same for all nuclei. However, the gradient magnetic field created different Larmor frequencies in space, according to $\omega_0 = \gamma B$. A Fourier transform of the signal will reveal all the frequencies in the signal. Those frequencies can be mapped to known locations, revealing a density map. For example, white matter has a lower T_1 than black matter in the brain. Since the white matter is located at a different position, the signal is encoded in the frequency. A computer can then generate the two-dimensional image, and even create a three-dimensional image after successive repetitions in different slices of the body.

For MRI, typical magnetic fields of 1.5 T are achieved in a space that the human body can fill. Therefore, large currents are needed to produce the magnetic field. The dissipation in regular wires would produce too much heat. So, only superconducting magnets can be used. They require constant cooling by emersion in liquid helium. Once the current is established, it will run without dissipating any heat; the power in an MRI machine is simply used to keep the helium cool.

The gradient magnetic field is applied in two directions. For the following example, we will examine only one gradient magnetic field, so that the magnetic field has the following form:

$$B(z) = B_0 + G_z z \tag{5.31}$$

it follows that the frequencies are given by $\omega(z) = \omega_0 + \gamma G_z z$. The signal will have the following form:

$$s(t) = \int_{-\infty}^{\infty} m(z) e^{-2\pi i \left(\frac{\omega_0 + \gamma G_z z}{2\pi} \right) t} \, dz \tag{5.32}$$

it can then be rewritten in the form that the carrier frequency ω_0 becomes clear.

$$s(t) = e^{-i\omega_0 t} \int_{-\infty}^{\infty} m(z) e^{-2\pi i \left(\frac{\gamma G_z z}{2\pi} \right) t} \, dz \qquad (5.33)$$

The function $m(z)$ can be obtained by applying the inverse Fourier transform. In reality, this is performed with the fast Fourier transform (FFT) algorithm. An image is then generated. Eq. 5.33 shows how the time domain is converted to space domain. A signal with more time, therefore will give more spatial resolution. For organs that move, such as the heart or lungs, complicated trigger schemes must be invented, in order to produce a long time signal for sufficient spatial resolution.

5.7 Quantum Computing

Quantum computing allows for very fast execution of parallelized code, such as prime factoring or sorting algorithms (Shor, 1997). For quantum computing, a qubit is the lowest unit and can be implemented in several systems, such as with quantum dots, ion traps, and NMR. The advantage of NMR is the long coherence time measured as T_1 (logitudinal) and T_2 (transverse) time constants. T_1 is also called *spin-lattice time*, or *amplitude damping*, and T_2 is called *spin-spin relaxation time*, or *phase damping*. in general, $T_1 > T_2$. A quantum computation should be finished before a state has become decoherent.[1] The implementation of quantum computing with NMR involves single-spin rotations (Vandersypen & Chuang, 2005).

Many books have been written about nuclear magnetic resonance. There are also online open-texts, such as Joseph N. Hornak, *"The Basics of NMR"*, http://www.cis.rit.edu/htbooks/nmr/.

---

[1] Some decoherence is allowable, since a so-called quantum error correction can be implemented.

5.8 Problems

Problem 6 - What is the nuclear spin I of the hydrogen atom, ^{7}Li, ^{13}C, ^{15}N, ^{19}F, and deuterium?

Problem 7 - How many possible energy states does ^{27}Al with $I=5/2$ have? What about ^{59}Co with $I=7/2$?

Problem 8 - Name three nuclei with zero nuclear spin; i.e. $I=0$

Problem 9 - What is the direction of the magnetic moment to have the lowest energy, which configuration has the highest energy?

Problem 10 - The Earth's magnetic field is relatively homogeneous over large areas. Calculate the resonance frequency of a proton.

Problem 11 - Calculate ΔE for a proton immersed in a typical B-field of 2.35 T. Then, determine the ratio of ΔE with $k_B T$ at room temperature.

Problem 12 - Calculate a typical value of ΔN for a system of protons at room temperature with $N=10^6$.

Problem 13 - Calculate the susceptibility χ. Note that the Curie equation is $M = \chi/T$, where M is the total magnetization. Express your answer in terms of γ and the constant magnetic field B_0.

Problem 14 - Explain why water can be treated as protons only in the case of NMR. And what about mineral oil?

Problem 15 - What is the resonance frequency of sodium in a magnetic field of 1.6 B?

6 Atomic Force Microscopy

A TOMIC force microscope (AFM) is an extremely versatile tool for characterization of nanotechnology (Giessibl, 2003). The AFM is a special type of Scanning Probe Microscope (SPM). In 1981 Gerd Binnig and Heinrich Rohrer realized the first scanning tunneling microscope (STM) at IBM Rüschlikon in Switzerland, which works on conducting samples by scanning a smooth surface at low temperatures with a Pt:Ir probe that is atomically sharp (Binnig et al., 1982). The probe is approached such that tunneling currents between the sample surface and the probe can be measured. Quantum mechanics make the tunneling current extremely distance dependent. Thereby scanning the surface at constant current a precise topography image is obtained. A few years later, the AFM was developed to probe non-metallic surfaces as well. At the time, Binnig, Quate, and Gerber (1986) demonstrated 3 nm lateral resolution and less than 1 Å vertical resolution. Nowadays, the AFM is used by scientists, researchers, and engineers for quality control and fundamental research alike.

After the experiment, you will be able to setup a commercial AFM, take basic topographical images, and analyze AFM images. The goal shall include a basic understanding of the concepts for atomic force microscopy and provide a beginner's tutorial for using the equipment.

This section will introduce you to some of the capabilities of atomic force microscopy, its applications in science, research, and industry, and detail the procedure to scan surfaces at sub-visible resolution. Visible light is an electromagnetic wave with wavelength $\lambda = 390\,\text{nm}$ to $770\,\text{nm}$. Therefore, features that are smaller than the diffraction limit cannot be easily resolved with optical light.

Nanotechnology has broad inter-disciplinary applications that include computing, data storage, health, energy storage, new displays, and bio-, gas sensor applications based on Gold nanoparticles, carbon tubes, self-assembly, and nanotubes. In order to understand and explore these devices, it is important to probe at length scales much below one micrometer. Atomic force microscopy is one of many probing techniques suitable for probing nanotechnology.

It is important to note that an AFM image does not represent the sample topography, but rather it is a convolution of the scanning tip and the sample topography. Each tip is nanoscopically different and therefore interacts uniquely with the sample. The interaction between the tip and sample creates the image. The image may also contain artifacts of the scan head (contortions), vibrations, interference of the laser, and the image processing.

6.1 Background

Surface morphology, electrostatic, and magnetic information at the nanoscale are explored using an AFM. The probing mechanism is similar to an old phonograph. In AFM, a very sharp (ideally atomically sharp) tip is dragged across the surface to measure a force of interaction between the surface and the tip. In vacuum, there are short-range chemical forces (fractions of nm) and van der Waals, electrostatic, and magnetic forces with a long range (up to 100 nm). In ambient conditions, meniscus forces formed by adhesion layers on tip and sample (water or hydrocarbons) can also be present. The van der Waals interaction is caused by fluctuations in the electric dipole moment of atoms and their mutual polarization. The van der Waals potential energy can be modeled as an attractive interaction with $V_{vdW} = -A/r^6$, where r is the distance between the two objects. Only at very close distances, the repulsive forces of the atoms play a dominant role; these forces can be modeled loosely as $V_{rep} = B/r^{12}$. The sum of these contributions is described by the Lennard-Jones potential

$$V_{LJ} = -\frac{A}{r^6} + \frac{B}{r^{12}} \tag{6.1}$$

proposed in 1925. The function is graphed in Fig. 6.1. The reader may be reminded of the contributions from van der Waals for the non-ideal gas: the excluded volume constant provides a short-range repulsive force that is balanced by long-range attractive force introduced in the pressure modification. Here, the van der Waals force is a short-range force. The origin is found in fluctuations of the electron cloud surrounding the nucleus of electrically neutral atoms. For argon gas, the constants are best determined to be $A = 1.02 \times 10^{-77}$ Jm^6 and $B =$

$1.58 \times 10^{-134} \, \mathrm{Jm}^{12}$.

In the case of AFM, this force is quantified with the Hamaker constant H, given the tip radius R and the distance r of the sphere from the surface, then:

$$V_H \sim -\frac{HR}{12r} \qquad (6.2)$$

with typical values of H in the range of $10^{-19} - 10^{-20}$ J.

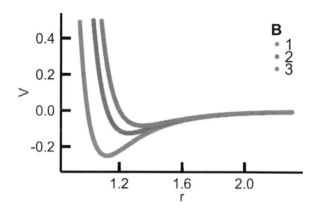

Figure 6.1: Lennard Jones potential for $A{=}1$ and variable B values and unitless distance r. The potential well models the sample-tip interactions. At large distances, the force is attractive (electrostatic), whereas at short distances, the force is repulsive (positive values). In non-contact mode, the AFM tip is operated at large slopes of the attractive regime. In contact mode, the tip is approached to the repulsive area.

In ambient air, surfaces are covered with a film of water. Therefore, as the tip approaches the sample surface, it will interact with water. The humidity of the room plays a role in the thickness (Butt et al., 2005). Sharp tips experience less influence from the water. A typical tip radius is about 8 nm, but varies with type and manufacturer.

There are different modes of AFM operation (static and dynamic are of main interest) with the basic idea of a feed-back loop that records the height, see Fig. 6.2. In static mode, the cantilever makes contact with the surface. In dynamic mode, on the other hand, the cantilever is positioned a few nanometers above the sample and oscillates at its resonance frequency. If the resonance frequency changes, the height

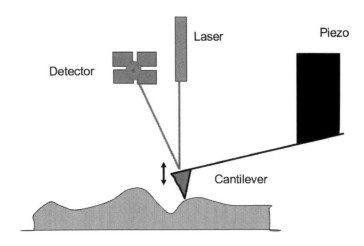

Figure 6.2: Schematic diagram of simple atomic force microscope.

is adjusted to keep the amplitude or force constant. The cantilever is attached to the AFM tip and the height is controlled with piezo-electric tubes. There are three tubes that are arranged to give full three-dimensional control, although only the z-control is shown in the simplified diagram. The interaction between the surface and the tip is measured via a reflected laser beam off the back of the cantilever. The detector generally has photodiodes that measure the light intensity. By comparison of the top-down and left-right ratios, the offset from the central position indicates the strength of the force. The piezo will then adjust the height so that the laser beam is reflected back to the center. The motion of the piezo is referred to as the *height*.

By rastering the image left-right quickly and top-down slowly, a topographical image is created. The image has a typical resolution of 256 by 256 points or more. It may take several seconds to several minutes to record an image depending on sample roughness and image size. The scan rate is reduced for larger areas. The maximum scanning area depends on the scan head and should be noted carefully, as exceeding the range could damage the piezo-electric element. For the NanoSurf EasyScan the maximum size is 50 µm, and for the NanoScope III, the tall scan head's maximum range is 10 µm. Before use of a new scan head, the piezo materials need to be calibrated.

The AFM tip, see Fig. 6.6, is at the end of a flexible cantilever. The

cantilever is usually an "I" or "V" beam depending on the required resonance frequency. The cantilever is attached to a larger chip (standard is
1.6 mm × 3.4 mm) in size. The cantilever is defined by a wet anisotropic
etch and usually on the order of 40 μm wide, 4– 8 μm thick, and has
a spring constant k of 0.1 N/m to 10 N/m. The resonance frequencies
can vary from 10 kHz to 300 kHz. For quantitative measurements it
may be necessary to know the spring constant of the cantilever. There
are several ways to measure the spring constant k (Proksch et al., 1996;
Gredig, 1998). The spring constant is related to both the geometry and
the material (Young's modulus). Two possible approaches include:

1) An approximation for a rectangular cantilever of width w is made
when knowing its thickness t, the Young's modulus Y and the length
of the cantilever l. In this case,

$$k = \frac{Y w t^3}{4 l^3} \qquad (6.3)$$

2) The image of the free vibration in air from a cantilever are due to
thermal vibrations. If no other forces act on the cantilever, then the
mean square of the amplitude $< x^2 >$ can be measured and using the
equipartition theorem, the spring constant k is,

$$k = \frac{< x^2 >}{k_B T} \qquad (6.4)$$

Such measurements are suitable for low spring constants and can
be made with an uncertainty of about 10%. It is evident that the
resonance frequency of the cantilever is a function of temperature.

Two similar tips will have slightly different resonance frequencies due
to microscopic variations of the cantilevers' shapes. The back surface of
the cantilever should be reflective, so that a laser beam can be bounced
off easily. Manufacturers often coat the back-side with Aluminum or
Gold.

The AFM image is always a convolution of the tip and the sample.
Therefore, using different tips (even if the same type from the same
manufacturer) will result in differences in the image. Some tips may
lead to strong artifacts in the images. So-called "double tips", for
example, result in images that have periodic duplicates of structures
or preferential directions in isotropic samples, such tips may be formed
after collision with the sample. If it is suspected that the tip has a

double tip, then it should be replaced, or the sample's angle needs to be changed. This can be done by rotating the sample, going to a different position, or changing the scan angle.

The AFM can be operated in different modes. The most common modes are called static and dynamic mode on the NanoSurf easyScan. The difference is in the operation of the cantilever. In the static mode, the cantilever deflection is measured as the cantilever makes contact with the sample. It measures the tip sample force $F = -\partial V/\partial z$, where V is the potential energy. In the dynamic mode the cantilever is operated at its resonance frequency (usually $150\,\text{kHz}$ to $350\,\text{kHz}$), where it the cantilever has maximum amplitude. A small force will change the amplitude and the piezo adjusts the sample-tip distance, until the amplitude is restored. This system can be modeled with a driven damped harmonic oscillator.

6.2 Driven Damped Harmonic Oscillator

The AFM tip in contact with the sample surface can be modeled and understood as a forced damped harmonic oscillator. First, the cantilever, as discussed earlier, has a natural resonance frequency owning to its geometry. Using the momentum principle (Newton's second law), we can write the differential equation for a harmonic oscillator,

$$m\frac{d^2x}{dt^2} + kx = 0. \tag{6.5}$$

The Ansatz for this differential equation is $x(t) = e^{\lambda t}$, which leads to the solution that $\omega_0^2 = k/m$. Therefore, the natural frequency of a cantilever of mass m and spring constant k is

$$\omega_0 = \sqrt{\frac{k}{m}}. \tag{6.6}$$

The temporal solution would be $x(t) = Ae^{i\omega_0 t} + Be^{i\omega_0 t}$, where the amplitudes A and B are determined from boundary or initial conditions. The damped harmonic oscillator has a restoring force that is proportional to the velocity, i.e. we can write it as $F_r = -\alpha v(t)$. The one-dimensional damped harmonic oscillator differential equation is written

$$m\frac{d^2x}{dt^2} + \alpha\frac{dx}{dt} + kx = 0. \tag{6.7}$$

This equation can again be solved with the same Ansatz, namely $x(t) = e^{\lambda t}$, which leads to the following equation

$$\left[m\lambda^2 + \alpha\lambda + k\right]e^{\lambda t} = 0. \tag{6.8}$$

We will set the first term to 0 in order to solve the equation. The quadratic equation has two solutions,

$$\lambda_\pm = \frac{-\alpha \pm \sqrt{\alpha^2 - 4mk}}{2m} \tag{6.9}$$

If we define, $\beta \equiv \alpha/(2m\omega_0)$, then we have

$$\lambda_\pm = -\beta\omega_0 \pm \omega_0\sqrt{\beta^2 - 1} \tag{6.10}$$

The solution can be written as follows and the amplitudes A and B are determined from boundary conditions,

$$x(t) = Ae^{\lambda_+ t} + Be^{\lambda_- t} \tag{6.11}$$

We distinguish three different regimes, namely

- $\beta > 1$: overdamped
- $\beta = 1$: critically damped
- $\beta < 1$ and positive: underdamped

Note that for $\beta = 0$, we get an undamped harmonic oscillator with $\lambda_\pm = \pm i\omega_0$. In the following discussion, the underdamped harmonic oscillator will be important. In this case, β is a small positive value. Commonly in AFM, the quality of the cantilever is measured using the Q-value, which is related as $\beta = 1/(2Q)$. Therefore, in the underdamped case, $Q > 1/2$. The solution for the one-dimensional damped harmonic oscillator is

$$x(t) = e^{-\beta\omega_0 t}\left[A_0\cos(\omega_\gamma t + \phi)\right] \tag{6.12}$$

The newly introduced frequency ω_γ is called the ringing frequency, or damped frequency. It is a constant. Typical curves for this equation are shown in Fig. 6.4. The maximum oscillation amplitude decays over time as

$$A(t) = A_0 e^{-\beta \omega_0 t}. \tag{6.13}$$

Using the solution Eq. 6.12 and inserting it back into Eq. 6.7, one quickly finds

$$\left[1 - 2\beta^2 + \left(\beta^2 - \frac{\omega_\gamma^2}{\omega_0^2} \right) \right] A_0 \omega_0^2 e^{-\beta \omega_0 t} \cos(\omega_\gamma t + \phi) = 0 \tag{6.14}$$

The first term will vanish, when the ringing frequency ω_γ assumes the following relation

$$\omega_\gamma = \omega_0 \sqrt{1 - \beta^2} \tag{6.15}$$

For high quality factors Q, the ringing frequency is close to the resonance frequency.

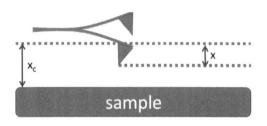

Figure 6.3: In dynamic mode, the cantilever is offset a distance x_c from the sample surface. The cantilever oscillates about the center position.

The AFM continuously delivers energy to the cantilever, so that we have a forced damped harmonic oscillator, which follows this differential equation

$$\frac{d^2 x}{dt^2} + \frac{\omega_0}{Q} \frac{dx}{dt} + \omega_0^2 x = \omega_0^2 A_{exc} \cos(\omega_{exc} t), \tag{6.16}$$

where A_{exc} is the driving amplitude. Notice that the electronic analogue is a LRC circuit. The battery is the driving force.

As the cantilever gets close to the sample surface, there is an additional force presence, and we can write the differential equation of a dynamic cantilever tip as follows

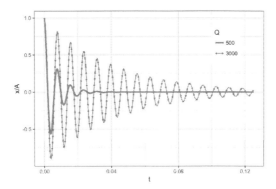

Figure 6.4: Damped harmonic oscillator's position as a function of time with $\omega_0 = 150$ kHz and $Q = 500$ or 3000. The lower quality factor means that the oscillations are damped more quickly.

$$\frac{d^2x}{dt^2} + \frac{\omega_0}{Q}\frac{dx}{dt} + \omega_0^2 x - \left[\omega_0^2\frac{F_{ts}(t)}{k}\right] = \omega_0^2 A_{exc}\cos\left(\omega_{exc}t\right), \qquad (6.17)$$

where F_{ts} is the tip-surface interaction and it is a function of the distance from the sample surface, so $F_{ts}(x_c + x)$. In order to remove the time-dependence from F_{ts}, we assume for small amplitudes the sample-tip force can be Taylor expanded. In this case, $F(x_c + x) \approx F(x_c) + \frac{\partial F}{\partial x}|_{x=x_c} x + \ldots$ and we can define a new spring constant k'

$$k' = \frac{\partial F}{\partial x}|_{x=x_c}, \qquad (6.18)$$

so that the equation of motion becomes

$$m\frac{d^2x}{dt^2} + \lambda\frac{dx}{dt} + \left(k - k'\right)x = A_{exc}\cos\left(\omega_{exc}t\right) + k\Delta x, \qquad (6.19)$$

here we substituted $F(x_c) = k\Delta x$. This is paramount to a shift of the resonance frequency by

$$\Delta f = -\frac{\omega_0}{2\pi}\frac{\partial F}{\partial x}|_{x=x_c} \qquad (6.20)$$

The frequency shift is proportional to the force gradient and not to the force.

67

6.3 Scanning Modes

Many different scanning modes have been established over the years. The most basic scanning mode is termed static mode, for which a stiff cantilever is used. The tip is in close contact with the sample. In dynamic mode, the sensitivity is increased by oscillating the tip at the resonance frequency at the cost of increasing the distance between sample and tip. Both modes are explained in more detail in the following.

6.3.1 Static Mode

The static mode where the tip scans the sample in close contact with the surface is the common mode used in the force microscope. The force on the tip is repulsive with a mean value of $\approx 1 \times 10^{-9}$ N. This force is set by pushing the cantilever against the sample surface with a piezoelectric positioning element. In static mode AFM the deflection of the cantilever is sensed and compared in a DC feedback amplifier to some desired value of deflection. If the measured deflection is different from the desired value the feedback amplifier applies a voltage to the piezo to raise or lower the sample relative to the cantilever to restore the desired value of deflection. The voltage that the feedback amplifier applies to the piezo is a measure of the height of features on the sample surface. It is displayed as a function of the lateral position of the sample. The cantilever can also be tilted left or right, this transverse data can also be recorded and provide additional information about the nature of the sample.

Disadvantages with static mode are caused by excessive tracking forces applied by the probe to the sample and from interference of the laser reflection off the back of the cantilever. The effects can be reduced by minimizing tracking force of the probe on the sample, but there are practical limits to the magnitude of the force that can be controlled by the user during operation in ambient environments. Under ambient conditions, sample surfaces are covered by a layer of adsorbed gases consisting primarily of water vapor and nitrogen which is up to $10 - 30$ monolayers thick. When the probe touches this contaminant layer, a meniscus forms and the cantilever is pulled by surface tension toward the sample surface. The magnitude of the force depends on the details of the probe geometry, but is typically on the order of 1×10^{-7} N. This meniscus force and other attractive forces may be neutralized by operating with the probe and part or all of the sample totally immersed in liquid. There are many advantages to operate AFM with the sample and cantilever immersed in a fluid. These advantages include the elimination of capillary forces, the reduction of van der Waals' forces and the ability to study technologically or biologically important processes at liquid solid interfaces. However there are also some disadvantages involved in working in liquids. These range from nuisances such as leaks to more fundamental problems such as sample damage on hydrated and vulnerable biological samples.

In addition, a large class of samples, including semiconductors and insulators, can trap electrostatic charge (partially dissipated and screened in liquid). This charge can contribute to additional substantial attractive forces between the probe and sample. All of these forces combine to define a minimum normal force that can be controllably applied by the probe to the sample. This normal force creates a substantial frictional force as the probe scans over the sample. In practice, it appears that these frictional forces are far more destructive than the normal force and can damage the sample, dull the cantilever probe and distort the resulting data. Also many samples such as semiconductor wafers cannot practically be immersed in liquid. An attempt to avoid these problem is the dynamic operation mode.

6.3.2 Dynamic Mode

In dynamic mode the tip hovers from $50 \, \text{Å}$ to $150 \, \text{Å}$ above the sample surface. Attractive van der Waals forces acting between the tip and the sample are detected, and topographic images are constructed by scanning the tip above the surface. Unfortunately the attractive forces from the sample are substantially weaker than the forces used by contact mode. Therefore the tip must be operated in oscillation mode so that AC detection methods can be used to measure the small forces between the tip and the sample by recording the change in amplitude, phase, or frequency of the oscillating cantilever in response to force gradients from the sample. For highest resolution, it is necessary to measure force gradients from van der Waals forces which may extend only a nanometer from the sample surface. In general, the fluid contaminant layer is substantially thicker than the range of the Van der Waals force gradient and therefore, attempts to image the true surface with non-contact AFM fail as the oscillating probe becomes trapped in the fluid layer or hovers beyond the effective range of the forces it attempts to measure.

The dynamic mode is a key advance in AFM technology. This potent technique allows high resolution topographic imaging of sample surfaces that are easily damaged, loosely hold to their substrate, or difficult to image by other AFM techniques. The Tapping mode introduced by Veeco overcomes problems associated with friction, adhesion, electrostatic forces, and other difficulties that an plague conventional AFM scanning methods by alternately placing the tip in contact with the surface to provide high resolution and then lifting the tip off the surface to avoid dragging the tip across the surface. This Tapping mode is implemented in ambient air by oscillating the cantilever assembly at or near the cantilever's resonant frequency using a piezoelectric crystal. The piezo motion causes the cantilever to oscillate with a high amplitude (typically greater than 20 nm) when the tip is not in contact with the surface. The oscillating tip is then moved toward the surface until it begins to lightly touch, or tap the surface. During scanning, the vertically oscillating tip alternately contacts the surface and lifts off, generally at a frequency of $50 - 500$ kHz. As the oscillating cantilever begins to intermittently contact the surface, the cantilever oscillation is necessarily reduced due to energy loss caused by the tip contacting the surface. The reduction in oscillation amplitude is used to identify and measure surface features.

During dynamic mode operation, the cantilever oscillation amplitude is maintained constant by a feedback loop. Selection of the optimal oscillation frequency is software-assisted and the force on the sample is automatically set and maintained at the lowest possible level (setpoint). When the tip passes over a bump in the surface, the cantilever has less room to oscillate and the amplitude of oscillation decreases. Conversely, when the tip passes over a depression, the cantilever has more room to oscillate and the amplitude increases (approaching the maximum free air amplitude). The oscillation amplitude of the tip is measured by the detector and input to the controller electronics. The digital feedback loop then adjusts the tip-sample separation to maintain a constant amplitude and force on the sample.

The resonance peak can be characterized by the Q-factor, which is related to the resolution. The Q-factor increases dramatically, if the tip is operated in vacuum. From the amplitude A versus frequency ω

plot of the cantilever around the resonance peak, the Q-factor can be measured,

$$Q = \frac{\omega_r}{\Delta\omega}, \tag{6.21}$$

where ω_r is the resonance frequency, and $\Delta\omega$ is the width of the peak at half its maximum energy. Note that the energy of the tip is proportional to the amplitude squared.

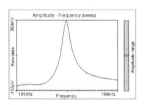

Figure 6.5: Frequency sweep of cantilever shows the resonance peak around 182 kHz.

When the tip contacts the surface, the high frequency (50 – 500 kHz) makes the surfaces stiff (viscoelastic), and the tip-sample adhesion forces is greatly reduced. The dynamic mode inherently prevents the tip from sticking to the surface and causing damage during scanning. Unlike static mode, when the tip contacts the surface, it has sufficient oscillation amplitude to overcome the tip-sample adhesion forces. Also, the surface material is not pulled sideways by shear forces since the applied force is always vertical. Another advantage of the dynamic mode technique is its large, linear operating range. This makes the vertical feedback system highly stable, allowing routine reproducible sample measurements.

The dynamic operation in fluid has the same advantages as in the air or vacuum. However imaging in a fluid medium tends to damp the cantilever's normal resonant frequency. In this case, the entire fluid cell can be oscillated to drive the cantilever into oscillation. This is different from the dynamic or non-contact operation in air or vacuum where the cantilever itself is oscillating. When an appropriate frequency is selected (usually in the range of 5,000 to 40,000 cycles per second), the amplitude of the cantilever will decrease when the tip begins to tap the sample, similar to dynamic mode operation in air. Alternatively, the very soft cantilevers can be used to get the good results in fluid. The spring constant is typically 0.1 N/m compared to the dynamic mode in air where the cantilever may be in the range of $1\,\text{N/m}$ to $100\,\text{N/m}$.

Summary

In contact AFM electrostatic and/or surface tension forces from the adsorbed gas layer pull the scanning tip toward the surface. It can damage samples and distort image data. Therefore, static mode imaging is heavily influenced by frictional and adhesive forces compared to noncontact or dynamic mode. With the dynamic mode technique, the very soft and fragile samples can be imaged successfully. Also, incorporated with Phase Imaging, the dynamic mode AFM can be used to analyze the components of the membrane.

If you run in dynamic mode, then it is necessary to find the resonance frequency of the oscillator first. In the dynamic mode the response is proportional to the derivative of the force F.

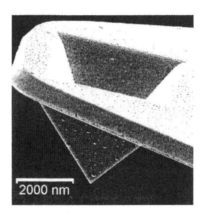

Figure 6.6: A scanning electron microscope image of a silicon nitride tip shows the pyramid at the end of the cantilever that is used for scanning.

The shape of the tip is very important in particular for magnetic force microscopy (MFM), where a magnetic coating is added to the tip. In that case the MFM tip may act as a magnetic dipole to detect the magnetic interaction forces.

6.3.3 Force Curve Measurement

In addition to these topographic measurements, the AFM can also provide other data. The AFM can record the amount of force felt by the cantilever as the probe tip is brought close to - and even indented

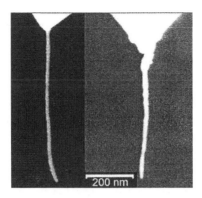

Figure 6.7: A spike tip has been grown in a scanning electron microscope by using carbon impurities in the vacuum and focusing them to the end of the AFM tip. The spike tip is from 300 nm to 600 nm long and can be coated with Cr/Co for high-resolution MFM spectroscopy.(Gredig, 1998)

into - a sample surface and then pulled away. This technique can be used to measure the long range attractive or repulsive forces between the probe tip and the sample surface, elucidating local chemical and mechanical properties like adhesion and elasticity, and even thickness of adsorbed molecular layers or bond rupture lengths.

Force curves (force-versus-distance curve) typically show the deflection of the free end of the AFM cantilever as the fixed end of the cantilever is brought vertically towards and then away from the sample surface. Experimentally, this is done by applying a triangle-wave voltage pattern to the electrodes for the z-axis scanner. This causes the scanner to expand and then contract in the vertical direction, generating relative motion between the cantilever and sample. The deflection of the free end of the cantilever is measured and plotted at many points as the z-axis scanner extends the cantilever towards the surface and then retracts it again. By controlling the amplitude and frequency of the triangle-wave voltage pattern, the researcher can vary the distance and speed that the AFM cantilever tip travels during the force measurement.

Similar measurements can be made with oscillating probe systems like dynamic and non-contact AFM. This sort of work is just beginning for oscillating probe systems, but measurements of cantilever amplitude and/or phase versus separation can provide more information about the details of magnetic and electric fields over surfaces and also provide information about viscoelastic properties of sample surfaces.

Several steps of the force curve as shown in Fig. 6.1

- The cantilever starts not touching the surface. In this region, if the cantilever feels a long-range attractive (or repulsive) force it will deflect downwards (or upwards) before making contact with the surface.

- As the probe tip is brought very close to the surface, it may jump into contact if it feels sufficient attractive force from the sample.

- Once the tip is in contact with the surface, cantilever deflection will increase as the fixed end of the cantilever is brought closer to the sample. If the cantilever is sufficiently stiff, the probe tip may indent into the surface at this point. In this case, the slope or shape of the contact part of the force curve can provide information about the elasticity of the sample surface.

- After loading the cantilever to a desired force value, the process is reversed. As the cantilever is withdrawn, adhesion or bonds formed during contact with the surface may cause the cantilever to adhere to the sample some distance past the initial contact point on the approach curve (B).

- A key measurement of the AFM force curve is the point at which the adhesion is broken and the cantilever comes free from the surface. This can be used to measure the rupture force required to break the bond or adhesion.

One of the first uses of force measurements was to improve the quality of AFM images by monitoring and minimizing the attractive forces between the tip and sample. Force measurements were also used to demonstrate similarly reduced capillary forces for samples in vacuum and in reduced humidity environments.

Concern with the fundamental interactions between surfaces extends across physics, chemistry, materials science and a variety of other disciplines. With a force sensitivity on the order of a 10^{-12} N, AFMs are excellent tools for probing these fundamental force interactions. Force measurements in water revealed the benefits of AFM imaging in this environment due to the lower tip-sample forces.

The liquid environment has become an important stage for fundamental force measurement because researchers can control many of the details of the probe surface force interaction by adjusting properties of the liquid. Experimentally, the electrostatic tip-sample forces depend strongly on pH and salt concentration. In fact, it is often possible to adjust the pH or salt concentration such that the attractive Van der Waals forces are effectively negated by repulsive electrostatic forces. This has been an important discovery because it can allow tuning of the liquid environment to minimize adhesive tip-sample forces that can damage the sample during imaging.

Atomic Force Microscopy has made its mark on a wide variety of applications as a topographic measurement and mapping tool. Now AFM force measurements are providing information on atomic- and molecular-scale interactions as well as nano-scale adhesive and elastic response. These measurements are beginning to revolutionize the way we quantitatively observe and, indeed, think about our chemical, biological and physical world.

6.4 PID Parameters

The feedback loop in the AFM is controlled with proportional-integral-derivative (PID) parameters. This is a widely used method to control signals. In the case of AFM, the amplitude $A(t)$ of the cantilever needs to be stabilized. The goal is to have $A(t) = A_0$ (constant) by adjusting the height position. We will compute the error signal $e(t)$, which is the difference between $A(t)$ and the desired constant amplitude A_0, or $e(t) = A(t) - A_0$. The height signal $\Delta h(t)$ to the piezo is now calculated as follows:

$$\Delta h(t) = Pe(t) + I \int_0^t e(t)\, d\tau - D \left(\frac{d}{dt} e(t) \right) \qquad (6.22)$$

In electronics, the P value could be the resistor, the I corresponds to a capacitor, and D is the inductor. The proportional gain P allows to control how fast A_0 is approached; the integral would dampen the overshoot, but if the oscillations around the set point A_0 are too strong, then the derivative D factor ought be increased for underdamping.

6.5 AFM Image Processing

There are several programs available for image processing of AFM images, see Table 6.1. Care must be taken, when loading the image, since

Table 6.1: Image processing software for AFM scans can be done with one of the listed software packages. The list includes

Name	OS	WebSite
WSxM	Windows	WSxMsolutions.com
		Ref. Horcas et al. (2007)
Gwyddion	Mac, Windows	Gwyddion.net
Image SXM	Mac, Windows	ImageSXM.org.uk
GSXM		
		Ref. (Zahl et al., 2010, 2003)
EasyScan	Windows	NanoSurf.com

one file can contain several images based on the recorded channels. For example, there could be one image showing the height and another showing the amplitude. The height image refers to the recording of the z-component of the piezo element, whereas the amplitude image is the rms amplitude of the cantilever. Strictly speaking in constant amplitude mode, the amplitude should be constant. Realistically, it contains the error signal of the z-component. Given the finite raster speed, the piezo element cannot respond quickly enough to keep the amplitude constant. Adjustments of the PID parameters, scan size, and scan speed can reduce the the contrast in the amplitude image, meaning that the cantilever tracks the surface more effectively. The quantitative analysis of the data requires careful calibration. The hysteretic effects of the piezo-element can even cause non-linear effects in the topography and overtime, the machine will get out of tune. Secondly, the image is always a convolution of the tip and the imaged surface, in particular for small scan sizes less than $\approx 2\,\mu m$.

As a first step, the image is "flattened". In this part of the image processing the background slope is removed. It obfuscates the contrast of the image. Even though it appears that the sample was flat with respect to the surface, at the scale of nanometers, there always exists a tilt. This tilt is removed by subtracting a linear slope from the image. Once, the image is "flattened", several parameters can be analyzed. This includes the surface roughness, the height difference between the lowest and highest point.

6.6 Height-Height Correlations

Images often contain small particles, the distribution and particle size is generally of interest. The particle size can be determined from the correlation function. In particular, the height-height correlation function $h(r)$ is defined as

$$h(r) = < |h(\vec{r_1}) - h(\vec{r_2})|^2 > \qquad (6.23)$$

the average square of the height difference between two points that are located at position $\vec{r_1}$ and $\vec{r_2}$. The distance between these two points is r. Immediately, it follows from the definition that $h(0) = 0\,\text{nm}^2$. Secondly, for large distances, as it approaches the image size a, the function measures the long-range roughness, $lim_{r \to a} h(r) = 2\sigma^2$, where σ is the rms roughness of the image. Empirically, it has been observed that $h(r)$ closely follows

$$g(r) = 2\sigma^2 \left[1 - \exp\left[- \left(\frac{x}{\xi} \right)^{2\alpha} \right] \right] \qquad (6.24)$$

where ξ is the correlation length, which is proportional to the average particle size, and α is the Hurst factor, which measures the short-range roughness. It is a value from 0.5 to 1, roughly (Gredig et al., 2013).

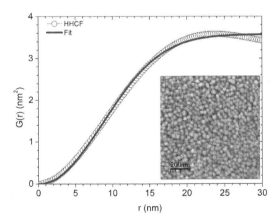

Figure 6.8: The inset shows an AFM image of a thin film of phthalocyanine molecules. The molecules form small grains. The height-height correlation function is computed and fit to Eq. 6.24 for comparison.

6.7 Problems

Problem 16 - Using the Lennard-Jones potential, (a) graph the energy for argon gas and find the equilibrium position d_0, (b) find a general expression for d_0 given A and B constants.

Problem 17 - Calculate the spring constant k of a diving board with length $5\,\mathrm{m}$ and width $1\,\mathrm{m}$ and thickness of $1\,\mathrm{cm}$.

Problem 18 - Find the dimensions for the commercial Aspire CT170 tip to compute its resonance frequency ω_0 and compare with the provided values.

Problem 19 - Compare the cantilever motion, a forced damped harmonic cantilever, with a battery powered LRC circuit. How are the inductance, resistance, and capacitance related to the spring constant, mass, and Q factor?

Problem 20 - Given the resonance curve in Fig. 6.5, find the Q-value of the cantilever.

Problem 21 - Graph Eq. 6.11 for the three regimes of β.

Problem 22 - What is the Q-factor for your tip (you can measure it)? Which kind of tip did you use and what is the resonance frequency?

7 Optical Photolithography

OPTICAL photolithography is a process of using violett and ultraviolett light to produce microscopic two-dimensional patters using photoresist. You will learn the processing steps that are involved in making electrical circuits. As your project, you will design, pattern, and manufacture gold lines from which you can calculate and measure the resistivity of gold.

7.1 Historical Background

The word photolithography comes from the Greek words, light, stone and to write. The pattern is then transferred onto "stone" or the substrate, usually silicon (Si), sapphire (Al_2O_3), or glass. The light interacts with the photoresist to create the desired pattern provided by a mask. Photoresist is a light-sensitive polymer. For IC fabrication, lithography is about 30% of the cost and usually a technical limiter (transistor size and performance).

Initially, lithography evolved out of the need to make photographs about 200 years ago. This lithographical process was developed in the 1820s by French inventor N. Nièpce. Commercially available pre-coated aluminum plates for lithography became available about a century later. The first silicon integrated circuit (IC) was fabricated in the late 50 s, about 10 years after the invention of the field-effect transistor (FET). Photolithography enabled fast development of electronic circuits based on silicon wafers, which had diameters of 300 mm earlier (and 450 mm after 2012). The wafer thickness generally varies from 0.2 mm to 0.8 mm. Each wafer holds lots of circuits and wafers are processed in batches of 25.

7.2 Moore's Law

The first commercial IC chip was introduced in 1959 and only 6 years later, the IC chip had 60 transistors. Gordon Moore of Intel proposed in his paper "Cramming more components onto integrated circuits"(Moore, 1998) that the number of transistors would double every 2 years (David House: 18 months). A modern chip, such as the Core i7, contains over 780 million transistors and is based on a critical feature size of 45 nm, much smaller than the wavelength of light. The critical feature size, or half-pitch length, corresponds to the smallest line width plus the minimum separation space to the next line divided by 2. Around 1985, this feature size reached 1 µm and is around 14 nm by 2015. Moore also foresaw that there would be a saturation point. Currently, Intel is developing 7 nm technology, by 2020, it is expected to have 5 nm feature size. This rapid (exponential) growth has led to unprecedented changes in technology over the last decades.

7.3 Process Cycle

There are several steps involved in creating a sample with a patterned structure. It is a cycle, because it may be repeated several times to create complex structures. In our case, we will use only one cycle. The fabrication of integrated circuits involves three main processes: a) film deposition, b) patterning, and c) semiconductor doping. This course will focus on the second part, which consists of several consecutive steps itself.

A process engineer (sometimes a physicist) develops a suitable process for the specific circuit. The engineer has several methods available, which will be explained. In the lab section, you will follow the "etch" process with a "positive" photoresist. Once, the process is determined, a mask is prepared. The mask is either positive or negative, depending on the process used. The mask can be in the form of a Cr mask prepared from a CAD design. Such a mask can have feature sizes of 3 µm to 5 µm. The Cr mask has a number of fixed patters and is used for repetitive designs. Alternatively, a mask can be designed with a simple paint program (InkScape) and printed with a ink jet printer onto a transparency. Ink jet printers are preferred over laser printer as they output more ink per area, which results in a darker region.

It may be necessary to overlay several transparencies in order to get enough contrast. The resolution is generally determined by the printer resolution.

A substrate is used to carry the thin film, which will be processed. The substrate needs to be very smooth, so its surface is prepared first. In the "etch"-down process, the thin film is then uniformly deposited onto the substrate. A spin-coater will deposit a uniform thin layer of photoresist, which will be pre-baked to evaporate the solvent. The mask is aligned with the sample, so that it can be exposed with UV-light. After a post-bake, the developer will remove some areas with the photoresist and show the underlying thin film. The sample is dipped into an etching solution, which removes the thin film in exposed areas. Using acetone or a strip solution, the remaining photoresist is removed, before the sample is ready for inspection.

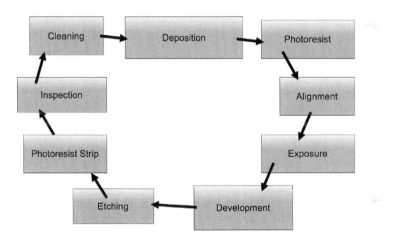

Figure 7.1: Lithography cycle.

The lithography cycle generally starts with the substrate surface preparation, see Fig. 7.1. The surface is coated via thermal evaporation, sputtering, spin-casting, or similar method. Then, a layer of photo-resist is spun on, followed by a pre-bake (soft bake) stage. The mask is then aligned and the sample exposed with radiation. The sample is dipped into the developer for a specific amount of time a given temperature and concentration. Then, a post-bake (hard bake) removes water. Depending on the process method, the films are etched and then photoresist is removed with acetone. The wafer is inspected and the process may be repeated for additional layers.

7.3.1 Cleanrooms

Air is mostly nitrogen and oxygen molecules. However, there are many small particles and pollutants floating in the air and therefore cleanrooms are used to handle delicate electronics. Nanotechnology is developed in rooms that have filtered air. The classification is based on both the particle size and number of particles per cubic meter. ISO Class 1 is the most restrictive cleanroom space. It limits particles of 100 nm and larger in size to fewer than 10 per cubic meter. In ISO Class 2, 10 times as many can be present, namely 100 per cubic meter and so on. In the ISO Class 9 room, which is similar to clean room air, there can be up to 35 million particles of 500 nm and larger, and almost half a million particles can be several micrometers in size.

Cleanrooms are ubiquitous nowadays. Since humans shed particles, like hair, cosmetics, bacteria, and so on, garments needs to be worn inside the cleanroom. Hair has typical size of 50 μm and bacteria range from 0.5 μm to 5 μm in size. The garment is also designed to be antistatic. It includes a hood, shoe boots, gowns, two layers of gloves, and face masks. The cleanroom is entered through a transition space to improve cleanliness. Extensive training is necessary to keep the room clean and understand how contaminants enter an area.

7.3.2 Substrate Preparation

The substrate is usually Silicon (Si), sapphire, GaAs, or glass depending on the application. Instead of sapphire, glass, or quartz are used for optical measurements. It should be noted that quartz does not absorb as strongly as glass in the ultraviolet region. The surface needs to be smooth, clean, and adhesive. Since air is filled with dust particles of all sizes, particles get absorbed to the surface; these must be removed. The surface also needs to be adhesive, gold will not adhere well to silicon; therefore a thin layer of Chromium (Cr) or Titanium (Ti) is generally deposited on Si first to form a layer to which gold can easily grow to. The substrate cleaning needs to remove organic and inorganic particulates and contaminations, as well as water. They can be removed with chemicals, ozone, or plasma stripping. Additionally, water can be removed by heating the sample or using alcohols. Care should be taken, such that heating does not lead to unintended surface modification through oxidation. The final layer of water on Si can only be removed at temperatures above 600 °C, however, upon cooling the silanol (SiOH) layer will swiftly reform. A common adhesion promoter is hexamethyl disilizane (HDMS), which can be applied by spinning, or preferably by evaporation onto a heated Si substrate. It is important to blow-dry the sample after preparation and not to allow the methanol or acetone to evaporate from the surface. This will prevent stains.

Fundamental understanding of physics can help in preparation of clean surfaces. Consider that metals will diffuse, therefore, if you heat a piece of Silicon wafer on a metal back plate that contains for example iron, the iron can diffuse through the Silicon wafer to the surface. At 1000 °C the Fe atoms have a diffusion speed of $D = 2 \times 10^{-6} \, \text{cm}^2/\text{s}$ and can easily penetrate a wafer of 300 µm thickness in $t = \lambda^2/D^2$ or in about 450 s. The opposite is also true, heating metals, or iron, will lead to strong diffusion of Carbon and other small atoms, which tend to make the iron stronger. So, heating an steel bar will enforce the iron bar.

A common cleaning procedure uses slightly warm soap to remove grease, fingerprints, bacteria, stains, and dust particles. The sample is immersed in a small beaker filled with soap. The beaker with the sample is then immersed in the ultrasonic bath for 10 minutes of cleaning. The beaker should not touch any of the sides of the bath and the sample must be sufficiently submersed. The water level of the bath should be high enough, so that it covers the minimum water level mark of the ultrasonic cleaning bath. This is very important as otherwise there is damage to the transducers, usually made from piezoelectric materials. Next, the sample is cleaned off the soap with distilled water. Next, the sample is immersed in a beaker with acetone for an additional 10 minutes of time in the ultrasonic bath. This solvent will remove many organic components covering the sample surface, and degreases the surface. Acetone is highly flammable and it evaporates rapidly. The small amounts of acetone left over on the sample's surface are removed with isopropanol and methanol. Again, the cleaning involves 10 minutes of ultrasonic bath in each of the two chemicals. Since methanol is the smallest molecule of all, it will be used last. In the last step, it is important to immediately dry the sample with compressed nitrogen gas. The sample should be used immediately to avoid contamination.

7.3.3 Thin Film Deposition

Depending on the process, the thin film or the photoresist is deposited onto the substrate. A thin film can be deposited using argon sputtering, or thermal evaporation. Other processes such as molecular beam epitaxy (MBE), chemical vapor deposition (CVD), pulsed laser deposition (PLD), or atomic layer deposition (ALD) are also possible. Most of these techniques require vacuum components as the thin films are slowly deposited. Since the deposition occurs layer by layer, it is important that only the intended material is deposited.

In thermal evaporation the deposition rate r_M is given roughly by the Langmuir-Knudsen relation

$$r_M = c_m \sqrt{\frac{M}{T}} \cos \theta \cos \phi \left(\frac{p_e - p_b}{r^2} \right) \tag{7.1}$$

where $c_m = 1.85 \times 10^{-2}$, and r is the source-substrate distance (cm), T the source temperature (K), p_e the evaporant vapor pressure, and p_b the base pressure in the deposition chamber. Also, M is the evaporant gram-molecular mass (g), so for Aluminum M=27 g and $T \approx$ 900 K. The angles are shown in Fig. 7.3.

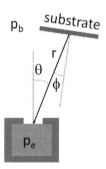

Figure 7.2: Thermal evaporation from a Knudsen cell with base pressure p_b and vapor pressure p_e of the material to be deposited. The Knudsen cell is heated to temperature T.

Since the container is also evaporated during thermal evaporation, an alternative is e-beam evaporation, where electrons from a filament are focused towards to evaporant filled into the water cooled crucible. This is particularly important for materials with high-melting temperatures, such as Nickel, Platinum, Titanium, Vanadium, and Tantalum, for example.

In the sputtering process, the target is not heated, but bombarded with Argon ions, the collisions produce atoms and atom clusters that are deposited onto the substrate. The target material is the cathode and the substrate the anode. The plasma can only be sustained in the chamber, if $Lp > 0.5\,\mathrm{cm\,Torr}$, where L is the electrode spacing and p the chamber pressure. The sputtering rate is

$$r = \frac{c_s}{Lp} \tag{7.2}$$

where c_s is a sputtering constant. The sputtering rate can be significantly (about $100\times$) increased by magnetron sputtering, using a magnet behind the target.

Layers deposited by sputtering and evaporation differ. In the case of Gold, for instance, the evaporated film is smoother as compared to a sputtered thin film. Typical deposition rates are $1\,\mathrm{nm/s}$.

The vacuum is needed to have a long mean-free path. The mean-free path λ of an atom in a gas depends on the density n and effective cross-section $\sigma = \pi d^2$ as $\lambda = \left(\sqrt{2}n\sigma\right)^{-1}$. The density n of an ideal gas is $p/(k_B T)$, so that we have the rule of thumb,

$$\lambda \approx \frac{5 \times 10^{-3}}{p} \tag{7.3}$$

where λ has units of cm, and p is measured in units of Torr.

7.3.4 Photoresist Spinning

A controlled thickness of photoresist is applied with a spin coater. Important control parameters are the spin speed, acceleration, spin time, temperature, humidity, and substrate geometry. Generally, two spin speeds are used. At first, the spinner is ramped to a slow spread speed, then accelerated to a higher spin speed. The thickness t is generally determined experimentally from known tables and is roughly proportional to the viscosity η and the angular frequency ω as:(Mack, 2007)

$$t \sim \frac{\eta^{0.4}}{\sqrt{\omega}} \tag{7.4}$$

Typical photoresist thicknesses are in the range of 0.5 µm to 6.0 µm. Lower thickness results in better resolution. Different photoresists vary in film thickness. For photoresist AZ 1518 the thickness drops from 4 µm at 500 rpm to 1.5 µm at 4000 rpm.

Photoresist is made from three components, (a) solvent, (b) binder, and (c) photoactive component. The binder makes up about 70% of the material. In the case of the Shipley S1818 photoresist, the solvent is propylene glycol methyl ether acetate, and the photoactive compound is diazonaphthoquinone. Upon exposure to UV light, the photoactive compound undergoes the so-called Wolff rearrangement and forms smaller ketene molecules, which are very reactive.

7.3.5 Soft Bake

The photoresist beads up at the wafer or substrate edge increasing the thickness locally. After coating, the film contains $20 - 40\%$ solvent by weight making a prebake (softbake) necessary. Baking the film reduces the film thickness, affects the development properties later on, improves the adhesion, and reduces the stickiness of contamination particulates to the thin film.

The pre-bake is done with a Fisher Isotemp hot plate. The top plate is ceramic and must be kept clean always. It is recommended to use a piece of Aluminum foil to keep the surface free of photoresist stains. On the hot plate, the temperature can be set by pressing the "Heat" key under the HEAT display. Next, use the knob to select the desired target temperature and press the "Heat" key again. The display will switch back to the actual temperature.

7.3.6 Mask Alignment

The sample and the mask must be aligned. Commonly, alignment crosses are defined on the sample and then aligned with the same crosses marked on the mask. The alignment can be made with a precision of a few micrometer. This precision is necessary to form several consecutive layers for devices such as field-effect transistors. A mask aligner usually holds the sample in place with a vacuum. Once the mask and sample are in the correct position, as verified using a microscope, they are brought into close proximity, within a few tens of micrometers. This distance is important, when considering the final resolution. The mask aligner also has an integrated UV lamp.

A simple mask aligner can be built by hand, using the schematics shown in Fig. 7.3. The mask can be printed with an ink-jet printer onto a transparency. The proximity of the mask and the sample is important, so it is important to understand which side of the transparency has the ink.

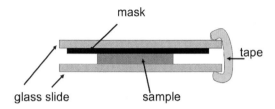

Figure 7.3: Simple mask alignment without a mask aligner is done using two glass slides.

7.3.7 Exposure

Photoresist can be activated with a specific spectrum of electromagnetic radiation. Therefore, the lightning in the room is important. Rooms for lithography are generally lit into the red spectrum, as development occurs in the high-frequency range towards the ultra-violet colors.

An inexpensive lamp is the B-100 ultraviolet lamp. It requires a 5-minute warm up period. The lamp should be left on, as the mercury vapor inside the bulb must cool for several minutes, before it can be turned on again. During the operation of the lamp, special UV-protecting glasses need be worn to avoid eye damage. The irradiance of the UV light is larger than that of the sun, hand protection should be used, when handling samples.

7.3.8 Development

Each photoresist has its own developer usually based on diluted tetra-methyl ammonium hydroxide (TMAH) solutions. The photoresist-developer pair determines the photoresist profile and line width. Sometimes two different photoresists are spun sequentially to form special undercut layers after development. The developer reacts with the ketene molecules and makes them soluble in aqueous solution.

There are two types of developers, metal ion free (MIF) developers and metal ion containing (MIC) developers. The latter have to be diluted before use.

Lower developer concentrations generally provide higher contrast, but take longer for positive photoresists. Negative photoresists require lower exposure dosage and lower developer concentrations.

Developers go bad through exposure to CO_2 in the air, frequent opening and closing of the bottle leads to lower quality of the developer.

After development, a post-bake (hardbake) takes place. It generally has a higher temperature than the pre-bake. If the temperature, however, is too high, the resist will flow and degrade the image.

Photoresist can be removed with acetone (wet strip) or plasma etching (dry strip). Plasma etching is more powerful as acetone may not completely remove all photoresist at times due to the high baking temperatures.

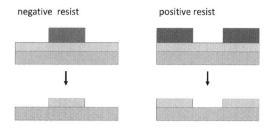

Figure 7.4: After development, the negative resist has the inverted shape of the mask, while for positive photoresist, the mask shape remains. After etching and stripping of the photoresist, the structure is revealed.

7.3.9 Etching

In a wet etch a strong acid is used to remove part of the thin film that is not covered with photoresist. In the simplest process, a metal surface may be covered with wax, then a pen may be used to remove wax at specific places. Immersing the wax-covered metal plate into an acid would then remove the metal in those places that are not protected by wax. Sometimes, a felt pen or marker is sufficient to cover the metal plate and protect it from the acid.

Gold has a very high density ($19.3\,\mathrm{g/cm^3}$) and its electron configuration strongly prevents oxidation. Therefore, wet chemical etching of gold requires a very strong oxidizer, such as aqua regia (mixture of nitric acid and hydrochloric acid), or aqueous solutions of the highly toxic sodium cyanide or potassium cyanide. There are also commercial gold etchants based on iodine which are cyanide free (less toxic), such as the Transene Gold Etchant with typical rates of $3 - 5\,\mathrm{nm/s}$. Agitation of the sample in the etchant solution will accelerate the etching rate. The etch rate can also be increased by a factor of 3 through heating the solution from room temperature to $50\,°\mathrm{C}$. The sample must be rinsed thoroughly in distilled water after etching away the unprotected gold film.

Etching away material can also be accomplished in the dry etch. This happens through the surface bombardment with ions. The sample is placed in a small vacuum chamber which is back-filled with a gas at low pressure (usually $10 - 30\,\mathrm{mTorr}$). The gas can be inert, such as Ar, or reactive such as O_2. In the dry etch, the photoresist may be hardened and partially removed. Special care should be taken, when removing the sample from the vacuum chamber, as there could be unknown fumes present in the chamber due to the reaction of the gas with the material that was removed.

7.3.10 Lift-off

In the subtractive patterning process, the film is first uniformly deposited onto the cleaned substrate. The deposition can be done with different techniques, such as oxide growth (oxidation of the Si wafer), chemical vapor deposition (CVD), physical vapor deposition (PVD), thermal evaporation, or sputtering. In the second step, photoresist is spun and then covered with a mask. Generally, an ultra-violet light source is employed to destroy bonds in the photo-active material of the positive photoresist. This part of the photoresist can then be removed with a developer. Now an etching solution is used to remove the superfluous amount of film deposited in the first step. Since the pattern is still protected by photoresist, the etchant will not dissolve those parts of the film. In the last step, the photoresist is removed with a strip solution. A patterned thin film will emerge.

For the following "lift-off" method, the substrate needs to be coated with a thin film. The thin film thickness is generally on the order of $10\,\mathrm{nm}$ to $100\,\mathrm{nm}$ in thickness. The thin film surface needs to be very clean of any contaminations. Therefore, it is always important to work with gloves as the grease from hands is very difficult to remove. Organic contaminations can be removed with acetone $((CH_3)_2CO)$, then isopropanol, and methanol (CH_3OH). The rule is to use shorter molecules later in the process.

Figure 7.5: Left image shows the developed photoresist on a glass slide; right image shows the etched gold substrate image overlaid with an anlysis from ImageJ to resolve the resolution.

The finalized samples are imaged and analyzed further with software, such as NIH ImageJ. An example in Fig. 7.5 shows the rounded edges that appear due to the lithography processing. The uniformity and edge size depend on the recipe used.

7.4 Electron Beam Lithography

For higher resolution, electron beam lithography is used. It is based on the same process, but instead of using UV radiation, the wavelength is much smaller. The type of photoresist is different as well. Fig. 7.6 shows a typical image of Cobalt nano dots that were written using e-beam lithography (Dumas et al., 2009). Even though the template had a square array of nano dots, the resulting image shows that dots mainly on the edges disappeared due to small changes in the exposure intensity and development process. The fine tuning of the recipe becomes very important.

7.5 Four-Point Probe

According to Ohm's law you can determine the resistance R of an ohmic circuit element by measuring the current I and voltage difference

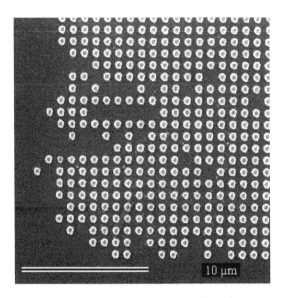

Figure 7.6: Asymmetric Cobalt nano dots with a flat top are created using electron-beam lithography. Each dot is smaller than 1 µm. The image is recorded with a scanning electron microscope.

ΔV given the relation $R = \Delta V/I$. In a 2-point measurement, the measured voltage will include the resistance of the wires and the contact resistance. Thus, it cannot be used for precision measurements.

In the four-point probe technique (Wenner's method), four leads are used. The outer two leads carry the current, while the inner two leads measure the electrical potential difference. This method avoids measuring contact resistance, which depends on the condition and material of the electrodes (Schuetze et al., 2004). Still care must be taken to avoid Schottky contacts when attaching the probes to the sample.

In addition to Wenner's method, the van der Pauw method attaches the leads at 4 opposite ends of the sample.

Temperature measurements can be made by immersing the sample into liquid nitrogen and then letting it warm up, while continuously monitoring the temperature and resistivity of the sample.

7.6 Problems

Problem 23 - Suppose Moore's law can be applied to the cost of cars and its fuel efficiency. Make two plots each with two known data points and extrapolate using Moore's law.

Problem 24 - What is the dot size of a printer with 600 dpi resolution?

Problem 25 - Derive the rule of thumb in Eq. 7.3.

Problem 26 - Briefly list and describe 5 vacuum deposition methods.

Problem 27 - What is an anisotropic etch? When should an anisotropic etch be used?

8 Arduino Interfacing

A RDUINO is a tool for interacting with the physical world through sensors. It's an open-source physical computing platform based on a simple and inexpensive micro-controller board, and a development environment for writing software for the board. It is an open-source electronics prototyping platform.

Arduino can be used to develop interactive objects, taking inputs from a variety of switches or sensors, and controlling outputs, such as LED lights, motors, and other physical outputs. Arduino projects can be stand-alone, or they can be communicate with software running on your computer.

The Arduino micro-controller is powered through the USB cord or with batteries.

8.1 Microcrontroller

The Arduino is a microcontroller with 6 analog in ports, and 13 digital ports. The digital ports can be either inputs or outputs. The microcontroller contains a microprocessor, memory or RAM, some flash memory, a clock (oscillator), and an A/D (analog to digital) converter. All of these components are integrated into a small chip, which is at the heart of the Arduino board. The common ATmega328 chip, for example, has 2 kB of RAM, 32 kB of Flash memory that can be programmed, 20 MHz oscillator clock, and 32 pins. This microcontroller costs less than USD 1.50, if purchased in high volume.

There are many Arduino boards with different configurations. These boards pack USB connectivity, built-in LEDs, power jack connection, and separate pins for inputs and outputs. Additionally, shields are available to expand the functionality for wifi, GPS, stepper motor control, and other features.

The Arduino is used for proto-typing and at the core of many Kickstarter projects. Recently, it has also been used in educational and teaching projects.(Esposito et al., 2015; Sarik & Kymissis, 2010)

8.2 First Arduino Program

The Arduino software is downloaded and installed from www.arduino
.cc. It comes with several sample programs that will be useful templates for further programming.

The first program that you generally run is the "Blink" program that will make an LED blink at the desired rate. The easiest program will in fact use one of the LEDs that is directly built into the Arduino UNO board. It is controlled via pin 13. The tutorial is available online at https://www.arduino.cc/en/Tutorial/Blink.

First, connect the Arduino board via the USB cable to the computer. Then run the Arduino software and compile the "Blink" program. It is important to select the proper "Serial Port". From the menu, choose "Tools", then "Serial Port", then select the "USB" port, see Fig. 8.1 You may also have to set the Board type, again in the "Tools" menu. Once setup, you can then transfer the program to the Arduino board, by choosing the "right arrow" button on the top left of the program, see Fig. 8.1.

Figure 8.1: Select the USB port from the Serial Ports, so that the Arduino program knows where to send the compiled program.

8.3 Serial Communication

There is a built-in library that supports serial communication with a computer. The Arduino board sends messages back to the computer. It is initialized with the command *Serial.begin(9600);* in the setup(). A number or text can be output with the command *Serial.println(voltage);*, where voltage is the measured voltage, for example. Make sure to use the proper quotation sign, if you are sending text as the compiler is very specific. Each line must be terminated with a semicolon in the Arduino C script.

8.4 Sensors and Physics

There are two aspects to Arduino projects. The first one, we will want to integrate sensors, such as the temperature sensor and convert the electrical signal based on the specifications given by the manufacturer; this is the engineering part of the problem. In the second part, the physics portion, we want to test the limits and ask questions such as, what is the resolution of this sensor, what is the response time, specific heat? How can the sensor be calibrated and tested for accuracy? For each question, we would build a hypothesis and a strategy plan for testing. We would then be able to quantitatively determine some of this properties, compare them with specifications that are published and add our own results.

8.5 Bot

A bot, such as SparkFun's RedBot, is a robotic platform that uses sensors to move the vehicle. The Arduino micro controller contains the code to analyze the sensor inputs and provide the commands to the motor. Two gear motors control the motion of the 3-wheel bot. The motors each provide a torque of about 0.078 Nm. By controlling the speed of each motor, the bot can be steered. In order to avoid obstacles and follow a path, sensors are used. The line follower sensor measures the amount of reflected infrared light and can detect changes from dark to light on the surface. It should be mounted about 3 mm away from the surface. It has 3 connecting wires, GND, VCC, and OUT. The GND and VCC are connected to the 5 V potential difference from the Arduino. The Accelerometer detects hitting another object or sudden vibrations.

8.6 Light Emitting Diodes

Light emitting diodes or LEDs are generally based on two semiconductors with different properties. One semiconductor is a p-type, while the other is an n-type. The charge carriers in the p-type material are holes, and the carriers in the n-type material are electrons. Each semiconductor has a characteristic band gap (forbidden energy region for electrons). By creating a p-n junction, current is easily conducted in one direction, but not the other. At the junction, electrons and holes tend to recombine and thereby emit light.

Due to the asymmetry of the junction, the LED has a cathode and anode, or a positive and negative leg. Therefore, it matters how the LED is connected. One leg is longer (anode) and denotes the positive end.

Depending on the wavelength of emitted light, the applied voltage for emittance changes. Typical values range from about 1.8 V for red light to about 3.3 V for blue light. Applying a voltage that is too low, will not be sufficient for recombination to occur and so no light is emitted. A voltage that is too large will *fry* the LED. Unlike ohmic resistors, where the current increases linearly with the increased voltage, the current in a semiconductor increases exponentially with the voltage. Therefore, applying a slightly higher voltage leads to a very large current that will become quickly destructive to the narrow gap in the LED.

Typically, for a diode, include an LED, the current - voltage behavior can be modeled with the following equation:

$$I(V) = I_0 \left(\exp \left[\frac{qV}{k_B T} \right] - 1 \right)$$

with k_B as the Boltzmann constant, T as the temperature, and q the charge of the carrier.

The Arduino board generally provides 5 V, therefore the red LED cannot be directly connected. The voltage must be reduced first. This can be done by inserting a resistor into the circuit. Part of the voltage drop will be across the resistor. For example, we would like to connect a red LED, such that the resistor will have a voltage drop of 3.2 V, such that the remaining voltage drop of 1.8 V is across the

Problem 28 - Compute the ideal resistor value put in series with a red LED to provide 1.6 V to the diode given an input voltage of 5 V.

Problem 29 - Discuss the temperature dependence of an ohmic resistor and provide a rough draft. Repeat the same graph for a typical LED. Over what temperature range, can you safely operate a resistor-LED circuit without providing too much current to the LED.

Problem 30 - Make a plot of the $I(V)$ function above for different temperatures and indicate the position of the value I_0.

9 Experiment: NMR

I am sure my fellow-scientists
will agree with me if I say
that whatever we were able to
achieve in our later years had
its origin in the experiences of
our youth and in the hopes
and wishes which were formed
before and during our time as
students.

Felix Bloch

THE background for pulsed nuclear magnetic resonance (NMR) is detailed in section 5. It is a testament of ingenuity in science that it is possible to easily probe the spin of a nucleus deep inside an atom. The experiment is based on pulsed and continuous wave nuclear magnetic resonance apparatus from TeachSpin. It has a magnet that provides a strong and constant magnet field to polarize spins of protons. The pulse generator can create a sequence of short RF pulses for adding a torque finely tuned to the nuclear spin. The signal is read out with the receiver coils and then amplified to be viewed on an oscilloscope. Given this setup, it is possible to determine the spin-lattice relaxation time and the spin-spin relaxation time of glycerol ($C_3H_5(OH)_3$) and other proton-rich viscous liquids. Secondly, you can determine the homogeneity of the magnetic field to high accuracy using the Larmor frequency of the protons. Finally, analysis and Fourier transform of the RF signal shows you frequency spectrum.

After carefully reading the TeachSpin manual, create a number of pulse sequences and view them with the oscilloscope (see section 9.1). Next, prepare a sample with glycerine or another viscous liquid, connect the pulse generator, amplifier, and detector using BNC cables, and then tune to the resonance frequency of the protons. The resonance frequency will vary every day as the magnetic field changes slightly with temperature in the room. After finding the resonance frequency, make a measurement of the free induction decay, all the time making sure that you optimize the position of the sample. At this moment, you can find the spin-lattice relaxation, at first using an estimation, and then by varying the delay time between the two pulses. The last part of the experiment will be the measurement of the spin-spin relaxation time. If time and interest allow, carefully map the magnetic field in the sample plane and determine inhomogeneities. In the following, details are provided to make these measurements. Keep in mind that it is important to understand the background from section 5 in order to follow the abbreviated steps. No attempt is made to provide a detailed and complete description of the steps necessary to complete these measurements, as the experiment should be completed in an exploratory fashion for optimal learning outcomes.

Goals for this section:

- Create Standard Operation Procedure (SOP)
- Operate oscilloscope to view pulse sequences
- Measure the free induction decay (FID) signal
- Measure the inhomogeneity of the magnetic field using the resonance frequency mapping technique
- Determine T_1 in a glycerine sample
- Determine T_2 in a glycerine sample using Meiboom-Gill sequence
- Write a Single-spaced 3-6 paged report (see Page 29)

9.1 Oscilloscope

The oscilloscope allows you to track very fast signals precisely. The Tektronix TDS 2002 has two or four input channels that can be displayed all at once or separately. You may be using a different model, so make sure to note the bandwidth and the sample rate. After powering on, you will need to wait a few seconds for the oscilloscope to boot, it will resume the configuration it had, when it was last used. The manual for the oscilloscope can be downloaded and is available online, familiarize yourself with the functionality of the tool before using it.

The oscilloscope shows time along the x-axis and voltage on the y-axis. The time dependent voltage signal is fed through the BNC connectors to one of the channels. Often short pulses that last on the order of $10\,\mu s$ need to be measured and cannot be resolved in real-time.

Therefore, the oscilloscope has an external trigger, which is a separate input channel. The trigger signal - sometimes also referred to as the synchronization signal - is generally a single short peak sent out at the time of interest. The display will then hold a short window centered around the trigger signal until the next trigger signal arrives. Depending on the trigger signal, the threshold or trigger level is adjusted to avoid false triggering. A good starting point to set the trigger properly is to use the "Set to 50%" button, which determines the maximum voltage signal from the trigger and then sets the level to the half point as the maximum voltage. The trigger signal will fluctuate a little bit.

The "Holdoff" can be used to set the amount of time before another trigger event is accepted; this can substantially improve flickering of the signal.

Data from the oscilloscope is stored using an external USB drive, which is automatically recognized once connected. Pressing the "save data" button will allow you to save three files, the settings of the oscilloscope, a capture of the screen image, and most useful, the data points of all the channels which are turned on. At this point, it is important to write down the filename in the lab notebook.

For each channel, the TDS 2002 will store 2500 points. That means, if you set the oscilloscope to capture a screen with $100 \, \mu s$, each data point is separated by $40 \, ns$, if the recording is at a rate of $25 \, MHz$. The estimate becomes important, when you are performing a Fourier transform of an oscillating signal as it defines the resolution necessary for resolving a particular signal. In the sample given, frequencies in the range from $2.5 \, MHz$ to roughly $0.1 \, MHz$ can be resolved. The CSV file should be used for generating graphs. A method is described in section 4.10.

Use the "measure" button to obtain data directly from the display. Use the "average" functionality to average over several signals. The "Single Seq" button acquires a single sequence and then stops measuring. There are many other useful signal processing events built into the oscilloscope. You can vastly increase the accuracy of your measurement by understanding the full functionality capability of the oscilloscope.

9.2 NMR Instrumentation Basics

A permanent magnet creates the strong magnetic field in the z-direction. In our experiment the z-direction is parallel to the table. The sample in the test tube can be moved in all three dimensions by using two separate adjustments. The planar position is controlled with two knobs from the yz-stage, which can be carefully rotated. The third dimension is adjusted with the o-ring attached to the glass tube with the glycerine. The magnitude of this magnetic field can be measured by tuning to the resonance frequency at each location. Since the Larmor frequency is directly related to the magnetic field strength, the resulting map provides insight into the inhomogeneities of the permanent magnet.

The second magnetic field is much smaller in magnitude. Therefore, a small coil produces the magnetic field pulse using the RF pulse generator. You can measure the magnitude of this secondary magnetic field using a test tube with a pickup coil inside. Using the geometry of the pick-up coil and an oscilloscope, you can determine the magnitude of this field. The sample will then RF radiate and this excitation is measured with a secondary RF coil through Faraday induction. The following components are used, find out where each of the following components are located and draw a diagram of how they are connected in your lab notebook.

1. permanent magnet

2. pulse generator

3. RF oscillator

4. pulse amplifier

5. receiver

6. linear detector

A block diagram of the TeachSpin apparatus is shown in Fig. 9.1. A permanent magnet supplies the field $\vec{B}_0$ along the z-axis (which in this instrument is not vertical but parallel to the table). The rotating magnetic field $\vec{B}_1$ is supplied by a Helmholtz coil with its axis perpendicular to the axis of the sample test tube. The field this coil supplies, of course, is actually linear, not rotating, but any linearly polarized field can be thought of as the sum of two counter-rotating fields. In our case only the component that matters is the one rotating along with the precessing spins. The other one can be neglected.

The magnetization produced by the sample does rotate, and because of this the receiver coil, labeled "probe" in Fig. 9.1, can be oriented perpendicular to the Helmholtz coil.

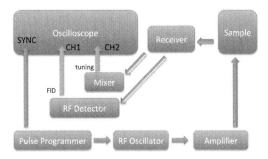

Figure 9.1: Block diagram of the pulsed-NMR apparatus used in this lab. In this setup, an RF synthesized oscillator is gated by a pulse programmer to produce, through an RF amplifier, an oscillating magnetic field $\vec{B}_1$ in the sample. Note carefully the orientation of the coils around the sample! As shown in this figure, the permanent magnetic field is applied perpendicular to the page; the applied magnetic field B is orthogonal to the axis of the sample tube; and the axis of the receiver coils is parallel to the test tube's axis. The output of the receiver goes both to a mixer (analog multiplier) and to tan RF amplitude detector (rectifier), and the outputs of these are displayed on an oscilloscope.

Read *2. TeachSpinNMR Instrument.pdf* for the individual components. You may want to have the file available while you are doing the experiment.

In particular, follow the precautions on p. 21 of the TeachSpin manual.

1. Please be extremely **careful with the magnet**, as described in the TeachSpin manual. Do not drop or shake the magnet, do not bring magnetic objects near the magnet, and do not drop magnetic objects in the sample probe. Do not force the sample probe past its limits of travel.

2. **Do not operate the power amplifier without attaching the TNC cable**[1] from the sample probe.

---

[1] A TNC (threaded Neill-Concelman) connector is similar to a BNC (Bayonet Neill-Concelman) connector, but instead of a twist it has a thread that is screwed in.

3. Do not operate the pulsed NMR unit with pulse duty cycles larger than 1%. Duty cycles over 1% will cause overheating of the output power transistors.

9.3 Prediction

Turn in the following predictions before starting the experiment.

Prediction 9.1. *Show a diagram of all major components of the TeachSpin NMR instrumentations and show how the cables are connected.* ∎

Prediction 9.2. *Make a graph of a typical free induction decay, where you plot the voltage versus time.* ∎

Prediction 9.3. *Show how you can extract the approximate time of T_1. Provide a step-by-step instruction set.* ∎

9.4 Exp I: Lattice-Spin Relaxation

9.4.1 Pulse Programming

Follow the step-by-step instructions in *3. TeachSpinNMR GettingStarted.pdf* in order to create several pulse sequences.

First, generate a single pulse. Set the oscilloscope time to 1.0 ms/cm and the repetition time to 10 ms and change the variable repetition time from 10% to 100%. What do you observe? Write down your observation in your lab notebook.

The programmer has two pulses which it can generate. The second pulse can be repeated up to 99 times. Change the A and B width, change delay time, change sync to B, turn A off, change repetition time, and observe what happens. Look at a two pulse train with delay times from 1 to 100 ms. Pick one condition and sketch what you observe in your lab notebook. Don't forget to make note of the delay time,

---

The TNC is superior in performance at microwave frequencies.

repetition time, and what signal you are triggering from. Also view the trigger pulse. How long is the triggering pulse?

Follow the instructions in "*3. TeachSpinNMR GettingStarted.pdf*" to generate several pulses of different widths.

9.4.2 Receiver Calibration

Supplied with the instrument are two vials with small loops of wire embedded in epoxy and coaxial cables connected to these loops. Notice that the two coils have different orientations. One is designed for measuring B, and the other is designed for generating a false signal in the pickup coil.

Read this section about tuning the receiver. You will need to tune the receiver to the oscillator frequency using a special *dummy signal* probe. Choose the appropriate coil configuration to do this measurement. Explain the rationale of your choice. Sketch the oscilloscope trace in your notebook when the receiver is tuned.

9.4.3 Measurement of the Permanent Magnetic Field

The first experiment we are going to do is look at the applied magnetic field B of the permanent magnet. Supplied with the instrument are two vials with small loops of wire embedded in epoxy and coaxial cables connected to these loops. We will observe B and measure its amplitude by placing one of these coils in the sample space and looking at the voltage induced by the oscillating B field.

Notice that the two coils have different orientations. One coil is designed for measuring B, and the other is designed for generating a false signal in the pickup coil. For the orientation of RF generating coil refer to Fig. 9.1. Which coil should you use to measure B and what is the orientation? What is the relationship between the voltage generated across the coil and B? What property of the coil do you need to measure to convert between this voltage and B? (This will just be a rough estimate, so don't spend too much time on precision here. An error of ±20% will be fine.) Clearly describe your procedure for measuring B in your lab notebook, along with the formula you use for converting your observed voltage to B and how you arrived at it.

If there are any cables connected to the front panel of the TeachSpin electronics bin, disconnect them and turn the instrument on. (The switch is in the back.) Locate the A+B OUT port, in the PULSE PROGRAMMER module. Using a tee, connect this to the A+B IN port on the 15 MHz OSC/AMP/MIXER module and then to the other channel of your oscilloscope. Trigger the scope off of the SYNC OUT signal, provided by the pulse programmer module. The blue cable attached to the sample holder with the TNC connector (see footnote on page 104) on the end of it supplies current to the Helmholtz coil. Plug this into the RF OUT port on the 15 MHz OSC/AMP/MIXER module. Also connect the BNC end of the coil you placed in the sample space to Ch 2 of your oscilloscope.

Because this instrument is designed for pulsed NMR, the RF oscillator is gated by the pulse programmer. When the voltage going into the A+B IN port is high, a signal is applied to the coils. When it is low (zero), no current flows through the coils, and no magnetic field is applied. The length of time over which the field is applied is set by the A-WIDTH knob on the pulse programmer module. On the pulse programmer module, make sure that MODE is set to INT, the SYNC switch is set to A, the A switch is ON, and the B switch is OFF.

You should now see both the gating signal (from Scope Ch1) and an RF signal (Scope Ch2) on your oscilloscope screen. Make sure your coil is optimally aligned, measure the amplitude of the RF signal you observe, and use this to estimate the magnitude of B. Estimate how long this signal should be applied to produce a $90°$ pulse. Sketch the oscilloscope traces in your notebook and include it in your lab notebook.

When you are done this part, remove the test coil from the sample space and disconnect it from your oscilloscope.

9.4.4 Larmor Frequency

The magnetic field strength of the magnet depends on the room temperature and sample location. Therefore, the precise Larmor frequency must be tuned every time and may need to be readjusted every half hour. Tuning involves the observation of beating on the oscilloscope. The beating pattern is generated by mixing two frequencies which are similar. The first signal is from the RF generator, which is mixed, see Fig. 9.1, with the receiving signal from the sample.

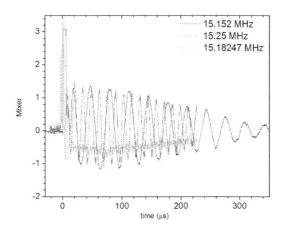

Figure 9.2: Beating patters are observed on the oscilloscope, when the RF coil's frequency does not match the Larmor frequency. Beating is observed both at 15.152 MHz and at 15.25 MHz. However, the beating is minimized at 15.182 47 MHz, which means that the provided RF generator frequency is the same as the Larmor frequency from the sample.

9.4.5 Free Induction Decay Experiment

FID (Free Induction Decay or Free Precession Decay) Use Glycerin sample for this part of experiment. Glycerin and mineral oil have similar T_1.

1. You have already done the first option in the beginning of the experiment. Skip this part.

2. Follow the setup. It is extremely important to find the zero beat condition. Turn on CW-RF (CW-RF switch must be off after finding the zero beat condition). If the oscillator is properly tuned to the resonance, the MIXER OUT shows no beat. If the MIXER OUT (Ch2 in the oscilloscope) looks like the beating pattern in Fig. 9.2, then the oscillator is not properly tuned. Adjust the frequency using FREQUENCY ADJUST knob in the 15 MHz RECEIVER module while monitoring the MIXER OUT signal. The zero beat condition is when there is no beating from the MIXER OUT and two traces in the oscilloscope are as close as possible. Sketch the oscilloscope trace of the MIXER OUT and write down the zero beat condition frequency. You can find a bit more information about this process in *2. TeachSpinNMR Instrument.pdf*.

After finding the zero beat condition, turn on CW-RF switch. Turn the A-WIDTH knob and monitor Ch1 (DETECTOR OUT). The short-est A-width pulse that produces the maximum amplitude of FID is 90° pulse. Sketch the oscilloscope trace of the DETECTOR OUT with 90° pulse, record the maximum amplitude, and measure the A-width.

Follow the instructions in the manual. You should be familiar with all the procedures in this part already. Measure the magnetic field in at least 3 x 3 points by changing x- and y-positions. Record the resonance frequency in the lab notebook. Show the calculation for the magnetic field. Use R to produce the surface plot of magnetic fields in xy-plane.

9.4.6 Spin Lattice Relaxation Time, T_1

Our goal is to obtain T_1 from Glycerin. Your group needs to produce a standard operating procedure on how to measure T_1. *5. TeachSpin-NMR Conept Tour.pdf* has useful information, so you should read that. Sketch one typical oscilloscope trace. Record your raw data in the lab notebook. Explain clearly what you should plot in x- and y-axis to obtain T_1. Obtain T_1. What is your error?

9.5 Exp II: Spin Echo and T_2

Our goal is to obtain T_2 from Glycerin. Your group needs to produce a standard operating procedure on how to measure T_2. *5. TeachSpinNMR Concept Tour.pdf* has useful information, so you should read that. Sketch one typical oscilloscope trace. Record your raw data in the lab notebook. Explain clearly what you should plot in $x-$ and $y-$axis to obtain T_2. Obtain T_2. What is your error?

9.6 NMR Lab Report

The lab report should contain several important results and features. Therefore, make sure the following items have been recorded properly. For one, you should have a free induction decay graph. It may be useful to also record the pulse sequence. Secondly, for the measurement of the spin-lattice relaxation time T_1, it is important to make measurements in correct intervals. The T_1 value should be extracted using a fitting procedure.

Problem 31 - Mix two sinusoidally oscillating curves with frequencies of $500\,\mathrm{Hz}$ and $501\,\mathrm{Hz}$, and compare the beating to another mixed signal, of $500\,\mathrm{Hz}$ and $502\,\mathrm{Hz}$. Include a graph with your computation. Discuss the differences.

Problem 32 - Compute the magnetic field for a Larmor freuqency of $15.182\,47\,\mathrm{MHz}$.

Problem 33 - Estimate the Larmor frequency change due to the change in temperature of $1\,\mathrm{K}$ around room temperature for a magnet made from Iron? How would it be different for Nickel?

Problem 34 - Draw a pulse with a pulse that has a rising edge.

Problem 35 - Draw a pulse train with rectangular pulses and a duty cycle to 20%. The pulse have $1\,\mathrm{V}$ amplitude and the frequency is $200\,\mathrm{Hz}$.

Problem 36 - What is a Carr-Purcell-Meiboom-Gill sequence? What is the purpose of the MG switch?

10 Experiment: AFM

> I lost all respect for
> angstroms.
> _____
>
> *Heinrich Rohrer*

ATOMIC force microscopy is a common instrument in many science
laboratories to go beyond the limitations of the optical microscope.
Nanotechnology is invariably linked with measurements and analysis of
features below the micrometer limit.

10.1 Prediction

Turn in the following predictions before starting the experiment.

Prediction 10.1. *Make a diagram that includes all major components of easyScan AFM. Show how they are connected with each
other.* ■

Prediction 10.2. *The height calibration standard sample is HS-
20MG. Make a sketch of the features and include a length scale.
Proposal 4 different images that can be measured with the easyScan
AFM.* ■

Prediction 10.3. *Estimate the size of a pit for DVD and for a
CD based on the storage volume. From that information provide an
estimate of the scan size.* ■

Prediction 10.4. *Graph the amplitude of a cantilever as a function of frequency with a $Q = 100$, and a resonance frequency of $\omega_0 = 200\,\text{kHz}$.* ∎

10.2 Exp I: Calibration Sample

10.2.1 EasyScan 2 AFM

We will use the EasyScan 2 AFM from Nanosurf to take AFM images. This device can measure the topography of a sample at nanometer resolution.

10.2.2 Setup

The EasyScan 2 AFM comes with a detailed manual explaining the operation. It requires three components. A computer for data acquisition, which is connected via a USB cable to the controller module. The controller module uses the Scan Head cable connector to connect with the scan head, a very delicate instrument. The Scan Head is placed on top of the stage using a tripod. The legs' length of the tripod is changed via screws.

Note: never touch the cantilever tips or any part of the cantilever deflection detection system. The cantilever should be approached to the surface with great care. After finishing the scan, the scan head must be raised sufficiently before the sample can be moved out. The Scan Head uses a laser to measure the cantilever deflection, therefore when turning the Scan Head around, make sure to always place the DropStop at the end.

Note: the Scan Head should always have a cantilever installed, otherwise the spring may damage the alignment chip.

After installing the system, inspect whether the cantilever is properly installed. Use either viewport on the Scan Head to inspect the cantilever.

10.2.3 Turning on the easyScan AFM

The software program is already installed on the computer. After connecting the controller to the mains power, switch the controller on and watch the lights on top of the controller to light up. Wait a few

Figure 10.1: The reflection of the cantilever indicates that the cantilever is very close to the surface. Coarse approach is finished at this point.

seconds for the process to complete. Next, start the controller software on the computer. A window will pop up and it will now communicate with the controller to initialize the components. During this process, monitor the lights on the controller. All the detected components will light up. If no scan head is detected, the lights will blink.

Choose the dynamic force operating mode. In order to find the resonance frequency, indicate that the cantilever is similar to "ACL-A". In general, you will be using an Aspire cantilever, which has a typical resonance frequency in the range of 160 kHz to 180 kHz.

10.2.4 Mounting Samples

Since there is sample drift, especially for small images, the sample needs to be mounted well. The sample holder is magnetic and can easily slide on the sample stage. Use a double-sticky tape to create a sticky area in the middle of the sample holder. On top of the double-sticky tape, add the post-it note. The sticky part should be up, so that the post-it note is secured with the double-sticky tape. Press down and make sure you have a firm and flat surface. The sample can then be mounted on top of the slightly sticky post-it note. Ensure that the post-it note area is larger than the sample area.

Add the sample using tweezers, then slide it over the stage under the cantilever. Take extra care that the Scan Head is high enough so that the cantilever has enough clearance above the sample after insertion. Use the three screws on the tripod Scan Head to lower the sample into proximity. At first use, eye the approach. Once you get close enough, look through the view port and identify the reflection of the cantilever on the surface. As you lower the sample further, the reflection and cantilever get closer as shown in Fig. 10.1. This is referred to as the coarse approach.

10.2.5 Measurement

For the measurement scan, the sample needs to be very close to the surface. Typical distances are a few nanometers from the surface for dynamic mode. After coarse approach (see Fig. 10.1), use the following sequence to start imaging:

- Acquisition → Frequency Sweep → Auto Set
- Capture the Fine Sweep (range of about $2\,kHz$) for calculating Q-value
- Click on "Approach", the green light should be on, "Approach Done" message appears
- Click on "Start" after setting parameters for image size, etc.
- Click on "Stop" to interrupt the measurement, and readjust parameters, or "Finish" for the last image

The finished images are automatically stored (although you can take additional images with the "Capture" button) until the program quits. Go to the "Gallery" to view the images and permanently store them on the disk. Make sure to use proper naming conditions.

The lights on the controller can be either red, orange, or green. If the light is red, it indicates that the scanner is in the upper limit position. In other words, the sample is too close to the tip. On the other hand, if the orange (yellow) light is on, it means that the sacnner is in the lower limit position. The sample-tip interaction is weak or the tip is too far away from the sample. It could also mean that the tip is not tuned, or the resonance curve does not show strong peaks; i.e. the tip is bad. The green light indicates normal operation. If the green light is blinking, then the feedback loop in the software has been turned off.

10.2.6 Improving Image Quality

The image quality will depend on the parameters that you choose. At the basic level, you choose the size of the image (*Image size*), the resolution (*points / line*), and the scanning speed (*time / line*). You can also select the scanning direction. Since there is a fast and slow scan axis in rastering and image, it is important to ensure that the fast-scan axis is not sloped. Invariably, at the nanometer scale, the sample will not appear flat, and you need to determine a good scanning direction by changing the *rotation* angle. If you have a step edge, it is advantageous, if the fast axis is perpendicular to the step edge.

In the *Advanced Level*, the z-controller's integral and proportional gain can be controlled. Depending on the size and speed, these gains need to be adjusted. See the discussion on PID on page 75.

10.2.7 Turning Off

Before finishing, you should make sure that all measurements have been saved. Be very attentive not to damage the tip as it is so close to the surface.

- Stop or Finish the image capturing
- Save all images
- Click on "Retract", which watching the cantilever rise in the viewport
- Use the tripod to carefully and slowly raise the cantilever to a save distance
- Remove the sample carefully and without damaging the tip
- Exit NanoSurf Control software
- Turn off power to controller
- remove the cable from the Scan Head
- remove the USB cable
- carefully store the controller and Scan Head in the suitcase

10.2.8 Adjustments

The image can be improved using several methods. The first method is to change the rotating angle. You can attempt to make the plane level during the scan. Additionally, you can adjust the PID parameters.

Due to the scan speed and the variation in topography, it is important to control the cantilever height precisely. However, different sample topographies require adjustments in the "reaction" speed of the cantilever. Therefore, there will be an error signal, which is defined as the difference between the cantilever height and the actual object's height. Naturally, faster scans are prone to increase the error signal. If you scan forward and backwards on the same line, the error may become very visible.

In order to minimize the error signal, it can adjusted with the proportional - integral - derivative (PID) parameters, see Sec. 6.4. These three parameters should be set in this order: proportion, integration, differential. Increasing the P-gain will decrease the error signal, whereas increasing the I-gain will decrease the error signal over time. The differential parameter is difficult to set accurately as it is proportional to the derivative of the error signal. All three parameters are explained in Fig. 10.2.

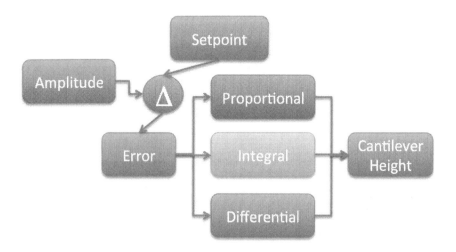

Figure 10.2: The difference between the amplitude and the setpoint is computed and regarded as the error signal. It is then processed through the PID and summed to adjust the piezo for the z position.

For good AFM results a vibration isolation platform is necessary. The vibration isolation consists of a large mass attached to springs. Between the low resonance frequency of the isolation system and the high resonance frequency of the microscope hardware itself ($> 10\,\mathrm{kHz}$), the AFM effectively comprises a band pass filter. This allows the user to safely image their samples in the intermediate range of about $1\,\mathrm{Hz}$ to $100\,\mathrm{Hz}$ and obtain good resolution.

10.3 Exp II: Data Storage Sample

On storage media, such as CD and DVDs, the data is written by indentation into a polycarbonate surface. The pits can be imaged with the AFM and several parameters related to the storage technology can be extracted, see Table 10.1. This includes the pit depth, width, pit

Table 10.1: Data storage recording media in comparison. Pressed audio records were available in the mid-19th century until the late 20th century, when the compact disc (CD) was introduced. Modern storage devices have capacities of 128 GB.

Media	Year	Size (GB)	Laser (nm)	Diameter (mm)
Vinyl Record				305
CD	1983	0.7	780	120
DVD	1996	4 – 8	650	
Blu-Ray	2006	25 – 50	405	120
BD-XL	2010	128	405	120

separation, and pit length. Use the results from the calibration sample to determine all four parameters for the sample provided. A laser beam is scanned across the surface and the reflection of a pit or surface is measured with a photo-diode at a rate of $\sim 1\,\mathrm{MB/s}$ for a DVD.

Data on a CD is generally encoded with eight-to-fourteen modulation (EFM). In essence, one byte, which corresponds to 8 bits, is stored as a 14-bit pattern. Therefore, a series with 14 zeros and ones corresponds to 1 byte of data. The additional 6 bits are used to make the data error-free and provide tolerance, if the reader is going a bit faster or slower, or could not read a bit correctly.

As a interesting separate experiment, you could determine the storage capacity by shining a laser beam of known wavelength at the CD, DVD or other storage media and from the diffraction pattern determine the storage density.

10.4 Image Processing

The atomic force microscopy (AFM) images are stored in different formats depending on the AFM vendor. Generally, these files include a header section that contains information about how the image was recorded, such as the tip's set point, scanning size, maximum height, PID parameters. This section is followed by height information for each pixel of the image. Generally, the height is limited to a resolution of 8 bits.

There are several programs available for Image analysis. The most commonly and freely available programs for download are:

- WSxM(Horcas et al., 2007)
- Gwyddion(Klapetek et al., 2016)
- Image SXM
- n-Surf Image
- ImageJ[1]

Once the image is loaded, the first step is generally to flatten the image. Since the image contains "raw" data corresponding to the piezosensor's output voltage, the sample surface is often not flat with respect to the head. Different algorithms exist to subtract the background, the most common being a "plane level" method. It uses all data points and computes a common plane level that can be subtracted. If there are a streaks in the image that were caused by a bouncing cantilever, they can also be removed.

The processed image can now be evaluated to extract different quantities, the following quantities are most relevant:

- surface rms roughness
- minimum and maximum height
- height bin distribution and symmetry
- mean height, average height
- autocorrelation length(Klapetek et al., 2016)
- average grain size
- height-height correlation length
- power spectral density function
- wavelet transform

The AFM is a powerful tool to measure the surface roughness; however due to the coupling of tip and surface care must be taken in the data's interpretation. Experimentally, Sedin and Rowlen demonstrated that there might be two different trends for measured surface roughness as a function of tip size as found in stylus measurements (Sedin & Rowlen, 2001). They showed that at small lateral scan sizes the image RMS roughness decreased as tip size increased. However, at larger scan sizes ($>5\,\mu m$) the roughness increased with increasing tip size.

It is widely known that most significant features of a random surface can be completely defined by two parameters: the height distribution and the correlation distance (Chen & Huang, 2004). For AFM measurements, we usually evaluate the one-dimensional autocorrelation func-

---

[1]for image processing, but cannot open AFM images directly

tion based only on profiles along the fast scanning axis. It can therefore be evaluated from discrete AFM data values using this transform:

$$G_x(\tau_x) = \sigma^2 \exp\left(\frac{-\tau_x^2}{\xi^2}\right) \tag{10.1}$$

where σ denotes the root mean square (rms) deviation of the heights and ξ denotes the autocorrelation length.

The difference between the height-height correlation function and the autocorrelation function is very small. As with the autocorrelation function, we sum the multiplication of two different values. For the autocorrelation function, these values represented the different distances between points. For the height-height correlation function, we instead use the power of difference between the points.

The height difference correlation function (HDCF) is measured as follows,

$$g(|\vec{r}|) = \left\langle \left(h(\vec{d}) - h(\vec{d}+\vec{r})\right)^2 \right\rangle, \tag{10.2}$$

where $h(\vec{d})$ is the height of the sample at position $\vec{d}$. The 1D height-height correlation function is often assumed to be Gaussian and can be expressed in this expression of Hurst,

$$g(r) = 2\sigma^2(1 - \exp\left(-r/\xi\right)^{2H}), \tag{10.3}$$

where σ is the long-range roughness for $r > \xi$, H the short-range roughness and ξ the correlation length. The Hurst parameter H is generally a number from 0.5 to 1.0 and describes the fractal dimension of the surface, where $D = 3 - H$ (Mandelbrot, 1983). The correlation length is directly proportional to the average grain size, usually by a factor of 2 to 3 (Gredig et al., 2013). Thus, the correlation function provides an easy measure of the average grain size.

The grain size can be further investigated using a Watershed algorithm (Gentry et al., 2009). This algorithm is implemented in the ImageJ software and can be used to create exact grain size distributions.

```
function [g]=heightDiffCorrelation(file,steps)
% (c) 2009 Thomas Gredig
%
% loads an image file and calculates the
% height difference correlation function
```

```
% (HDCF) g(r)
%
% g(r) = <h(x,y) - h(x',y')>, for all x,y where
% r=sqrt((x-x')^2-(y-y')^2)
%
% use Monte Carlo - like approach
% file - name of image file, must be square
% steps - how many steps in calculation

A=imread(file);
% must be grey scale image

lenA=length(A)-1;
c=abs(lenA*0.5);
g=zeros(lenA+c,1);
f=zeros(lenA+c,1);
i=0;

while i<steps
    pos = round(rand(2)*lenA+1);
    dist = round(sqrt((pos(1,1)-pos(1,2))^2+
                     (pos(2,1)-pos(2,2))^2));
    n=abs(double(A(pos(1,1),pos(2,1)))-
          double(A(pos(1,2),pos(2,2))));
    g(dist)=g(dist)+n;
    f(dist)=f(dist)+1;
    i=i+1;
end

for j=1:lenA+c
    if f(j)>0
        g(j)=g(j)/f(j);
    end
end
```

10.5 Related Techniques

There is a wide range of scanning methods that are based on a similar principle as atomic force microscopy. The most common is scanning tunneling microscopy (STM) which can resolve individual atoms. The surface needs to be conductive, so that a current can run from the sharp tip to the sample. Where the tip and the sample meet, there is a tunnel junction. Since the tunneling current depends exponentially on distance, precise z-resolution is achieved. Even atomic resolution can

120

be achieved for atomically flat samples. Tunneling currents are small usually ~ 100pA and need to be amplified. Two common modes of operation are used a) constant height and b) constant current.

10.6 AFM Lab Report

The AFM lab report includes an image of the calibration sample and analyzes the height and width using line profiles. In the second part, an image of the storage device is shown. Discuss the data density that you obtain from the AFM images. You may also discuss how the shape of the trenches that you found, and provide a histogram of the lengths.

10.7 Problems

Problem 37 - Small nano-spheres of 50 nm diameter are randomly deposited on a perfectly flat substrate. Discuss various possibilities of what you observe with an AFM tip depending on the density of spheres. Assume that the tip has a curvature of 20 nm and is otherwise shaped like a pyramid. Draw a line trace that shows the spheres and the AFM tip as it traces the surface.

Problem 38 - PID parameters are often used to control the temperature, say an oven uses a PID controller to set the temperature above room temperature. Draw what happens to the temperature as a function of time for a large (mass) oven with a small heater that has both I and D set to 0 and only uses P.

Problem 39 - What are autocorrelation functions? How is the autocorrelation length computed? What is the meaning of the auto-correlation length?

Problem 40 - Calculate the total length of pits on a typical DVD.

Problem 41 - Estimate the amount of data you could store on a vinyl record disk using digital encoding.

11 Experiment: Lithography

> I had no idea this was going
> to be an accurate prediction,
> but amazingly enough instead
> of 10 [years] doubling, we got
> nine over the 10 years, but
> still followed pretty well along
> the curve.
>
> *Gordon Moore*

PHOTOLITHOGRAPHY is the standard method for printing circuits
and microprocessor fabrication. The process of lithography is similar to film development in a dark room. This skill is commonly used by researchers, process engineers, research scientists, equipment supervisors, designers, application engineers, and material scientists. In biology and biochemistry, soft lithography is used control the surface structure, pattern complex molecules relevant to biology.

The central purpose of this experiment is to explore the photolithography process through (a) designing a mask, (b) transferring the mask onto a gold-coated glass slide, (c) etch the pattern, and (d) determine thickness of the gold film.

11.1 Mask Design

You will be given a glass slide of size $\sim 25 \times 25 \, \text{mm}^2$. It will be coated with nanometer thick layer of gold. Design a mask following the criteria below.

The design of the mask will be created using the program *InkScape* in black and white. InkScape allows you to define the size in mm, so that the print-out will have the exact dimensions needed. Once the mask is designed, it will be printed on a transparency. The transparency will then be the mask for the photolithography project. From the InkScape menu, choose File → Properties and set the size to $25 \times 25\,mm^2$, also change the default units to *mm* inside the Properties menu.

- For this gold thickness, compute the minimum length and width of a gold wire, so that the resistance is at least $10\,\Omega$.
- Create wires that are at least $0.8\,mm$ wide and have different lengths. Wires that are narrower will require advanced knowledge in lithography processing.
- There should be several pads, such that you can measure a minimum of 10 different lengths. Note that the pad needs to be much larger than the wire width. It should be at least $4 \times 4\,mm^2$, but $5 \times 5\,mm^2$ is better, so that you can easily make contact. Note that one wire with 4 pads allows you to measure 6 different lengths. How is that?
- The wires should be designed such that the resistance is $10\,\Omega$ or more.
- The design should optimize the pattern to allow for errors in the process. Edges may have problems, so the entire device should not suffer due to one missing area, for example. Your design should probably have a $1\,mm$ edge and small features need to be on the inside, larger features on the outside.
- Additionally, the mask should allow you to make a 4-point probe measurement. Discuss how it works and what the advantages are.
- Make a prediction of the length and the resistance. Make a plot that shows where the predicted data points should be for your mask. The x-axis of the plot is the gold wire length and the y-axis is the resistance.

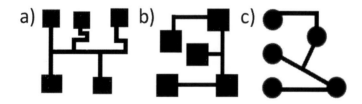

Figure 11.1: Three examples of Au circuits with pads for measurements.

11.2 Prediction

Turn in the following predictions before starting the experiment.

> **Prediction 11.1.** *Compute the resistance of a* 5 mm *long Gold wire with diameter* 1 μm. ■

> **Prediction 11.2.** *Design a mask no larger than* 25×25 mm², *then print out on on a transparency. More details are included in Sec. 11.1.* ■

> **Prediction 11.3.** *Predict the resistances of all pathways on your mask for a thin film of Gold with thickness* 30 nm. ■

11.3 Exp I: Recipe Optimization

A recipe needs to be created for each new fabrication design. It will depend on many factors, including the age and viscosity of the chemicals used. Here are typical values that can be used with the Shipley AZ1512 (or S1818) positive photoresist:

- carefully clean substrates with acetone, isopropanol, methanol in ultrasonic bath
- dispense AZ1512, spin 40 s at 4000 rpm
- softbake 60 s at 95 °C
- expose 30 s under UV light
- develop for 20 s, agitate, and rinse thoroughly in DI water
- blow dry at angle with N_2 gun
- hardbake 60 s at 115 °C
- etch Au for 3 s to 9 s, check periodically
- remove resist with acetone
- inspect sample
- clean-up

The operation of the spin coater is detailed in the WS-400/500B Lite series spin processor operation manual from Laurell Technologies Corporation. You should note that you need to establish a vacuum to keep the sample steady during the fast spinning operation. House vacuum will be used (yellow knob on fume hood). Secondly, the machine needs at least 60 psi (4.1 bar) of nitrogen to pressurize the motor seal. This is crucial to keep the electronics and electronics from being contaminated. Therefore, you must ensure that there is a nitrogen flow during the operation of the unit.

The microprocessor control can be programmed to perform the spin-coating process. The essential parameters are the spinning speed and the spinning time. For more advanced configuration, acceleration, deceleration can also be programmed, and multi-step speed programs can be setup. Each program is assigned a letter, so that they can easily be recalled.

Important, the lid needs to be closed, before you start the spin processing, otherwise chemicals can be sprayed uncontrollably. Also, importantly the sample needs to cover the rubber sealing ring completely; i.e. the sample needs to be sufficiently larger than the rubber sealing ring to absolutely prevent any photoresist being sucked into the vacuuming system.

The compressed gas cylinder uses a very high pressure (up to 2500 psi) to store the gas. Knocking off the top of the cylinder would have so much gas mass being released that the cylinder can act like a projectile, see O_2 Cylinder Rocket Mythbuster experiment. Therefore, care must be taken. The pressure is down-regulated using a gas regulator. The regulator is set at more than 60 psi and should not be changed. Rather, only the valves are slowly opened to make the gas stream.

Please note that the UV light lamp projects light in the ultra-violet regime, therefore it is not visible. Glasses that protect you from UV light should be worn. Also, minimize direct exposure to skin, such as hands, when placing and removing the sample.

11.3.1 Cleanup

The last step includes the inspection of the sample. Once, a good sample has been made, the process has been established. The cleaning includes removing all photoresist from the contaminated parts (spin-coater, glassware, etc.). It is of utter importance to be careful that your skin does not come into direct contact with the photoresist and therefore cleaning all contaminated surfaces carefully is an important last step. Photoresist comes off with acetone. Use wipes and soak them in slightly in acetone, then wipe the surfaces. Make sure that you do not wipe any rubber parts with acetone, as the acetone will make rubber brittle and eventually break the rubber ring. Also, make sure to not wipe plexiglass surfaces (top of spin-coater) as plexiglass acrylic will cloud permanently if in contact with acetone.

11.4 Exp II: Resistance Measurements

Resistance can be measured with a 2-point or 4-point measurement. The 4-point measurement is much more accurate as it provides current separately in two channels and measures the voltage difference between two points separately.

11.4.1 Etching

The etching solution is is called Gold Etchant TFA made by Transene Company, Inc. and it is based on KI-I_2 complex. The etching should be done inside a ventilated hood. The rate will be roughly 3 nm/s at room temperature. The rate can be doubled if the etchant temperature is raised to 45 °C. After etching, the sample should be thoroughly rinsed in distilled water. The waste product needs to be disposed in accordance with state regulations in an approved waste disposal facility.

11.5 Lithography Report

The lithography report includes the mask design and computed values for the resistance. It provides a detailed report on the optimized procedure that was used to build the mask. A graph of the length versus resistance will compare the actual resistance values with the predicted values for a given thickness. Extract the gold thickness, if possible. Discuss any assumptions. Finally, investigate the feature size using optical images of your final device with the ImageJ software.

assumptions.

Problem 42 - What would be the best resolution you could get with a 720 dpi printer?

Problem 43 - A particular photoresist is spin coated and yields a $3\,\mu m$ thick layer. If you were to double the speed, what thickness would you expect?

Problem 44 - Compute the resistance of a Gold wire that is $50\,nm$ thick and $10\,mm$ long, as well as (a) $800\,\mu m$ wide. (b) Photolithography may yield wires with variable widths. Compute the resistance again, if the the width of the wire varies between $600\,\mu m$ to $800\,\mu m$. Provide your model and

Problem 45 - Given a $20\,nm$ thick gold film and a $\sim 25\times 25\,mm^2$ substrate with $0.8\,mm$ minimum feature size and two $\sim 4\times 4\,mm^2$-sized measurement pads, what is the maximum resistance for the longest possible wire that you can design?

Problem 46 - If the horizontal maximum distance of each of the sketches in Fig. 11.1 is $23\,mm$, then calculate the expected resistance for a Gold film of $40\,nm$ thickness for all possible paths of one selected device. Provide a diagram and label all pads. Discuss any assumptions that you make.

128

12 Experiment: Arduino

> I argue there is another revolution going on, and it is the one that has to do with the open-source hardware and maker's movement.
>
> *Massimo Banzi*

IN the first step, establish that the Arduino components work and interact in a controllable way. Therefore, the first part of the experiment will introduce you to the micro-controller and how it is programmed using the Arduino language. In the second part, you will perform a typical physics experiment using the Arduino components and sensor to efficiently and accurately collect data. The proposed experiment has to do with heat absorption of two objects made of the same material, but different color. If possible, you should add an extension to the experiment that would solidify our physics knowledge.

12.1 First Steps

If you are not familiar or only minimally with the Arduino micro-controller, then follow this exercise. In this introduction project, connect a resistor and LED in series. Make sure that the LED's polarity is connected properly. Also make sure - see earlier discussion - that you choose the correct resistance. Use Pin 12 to control whether the LED is on or off. Simply connect the positive end of the LED to Pin 12 and the end of the resistor to the ground (GND). Note that you will break the LED, if you connect the negative end to the ground as you would then provide 5 V to a LED, which operates on about 2 V; that is the reason for the resistor.

Now, use the code to set Pin 12 to either a high state (5 V), or a low state (0 V); since in the low state, there is no potential difference, there the LED will be off. Copy the code from Listing 12.1.

Arduino programming language is similar to the C language. The programs are very small and the commands are limited. If you are know programming, it will be easy to learn, and if you are new to programming, this may be an ideal introduction due to its limitations. In the text here, we will assume no or very limited programming knowledge.

The Arduino software is open-source and works on all major computing platforms. It is downloaded from `https://www.arduino.cc/en/Main/Software`.

The Arduino controller will initialize and then execute the **setup()** sequence once. It must be named exactly so. Words which are printed in bold in the Listing 12.1 cannot be altered and have a specific meaning. Upper and lowercase also matter. Use the curly brackets to define the scope of this function. The second function that must be implemented is called **loop()**. After the setup, the loop function will be executed and repeated forever as long as the Arduino board has power. In order to slow down the execution of the code, you can use the function **delay()**, which will do nothing for a given time specified as an integer in units of ms.

When numbers are stored in variables, they can be stored in either an **int** or **float**. Variable names are up to you and are not printed in bold, such as the variable celsius in Listing 12.2. The difference is that int can only store whole numbers; i.e. integers. The float can store decimals. Therefore, 2.0 is automatically a float and 2 is an integer. The storage of numbers in integers uses less memory.

Listing 12.1: Arduino code to make an LED connected to pin 12 blink. The short leg of the LED needs to be connected to a resistor, which is connected to the ground.

```
  void setup() {
    pinMode(12, OUTPUT);
  }

5 void loop() {
    digitalWrite(12, HIGH);
    delay(500);
    digitalWrite(12, LOW);

10   // wait for 1000 ms
    delay(1000);
  }
```

12.2 Prediction

Turn in the following predictions before starting the experiment.

12.3 Exp I: Hand Motion Controller

The goal of this experiment is to determine the angular resolution of a flex sensor. First, create a circuit and program with the Arduino micro controller that will turn on an LED, if a flex sensor is bent beyond a particular angle. The LED should be off, when the sensor is straight, and on when the sensor is bent. Remember that the LED has a polarity, and also remember that the maximum voltage that can deliver to an LED is 2 V; therefore, you have to limit the voltage that the board outputs.

Devise a method to measure and quantify the angle or bend of the flex sensor. There are many ways to quantify the bending of the sensor. Using a phone to image the sensor's position may provide important data. Measure the resistance as a function of your newly defined quantity and create a detailed graph. You should measure reversibility and note any hysteretic effects. Secondly, probe any limitations as to the resolution to the bend angle that can be detected, any time effects, hysteretic effects. Finally, compare your results with the results available from the manufacturer. Reflect on developing a wearable glove, where the fingers' motion is detected using flex sensors.

Optionally, replace the LED with a servo motor or the piezo buzzer and control motor speed or sound frequency using the flex sensor.

12.3.1 Flex Sensor

The flex sensor has only two inputs. It acts as a resistor. The value of the resistance is measured with a voltage divider; i.e. a circuit with the the flex sensor is put in series and connected to the 5 V output. Reading the voltage split, it is possible to determine the resistance of the flex sensor.

12.4 Exp II: Blackbody Radiation

There are several low-cost temperature sensors for the Arduino micro-controller. The simple TMP36GZ temperature sensor has three pins. The pins correspond to ground (V_{gnd}), the measured output voltage (V_{out}), and the source voltage (V_s). It is important to identify the proper grounding pinThe operating source voltage can be 2.7 V to 5.5 V. The output voltage is proportional to the temperature in units of °C.

If the leads to the temperature sensor are long, then you should use a capacitor of approximate size 0.1 μF. Note that the time constant for A capacitor that is connected between the V_s and the ground will smooth the supply of the voltage. You can also add the capacitor between the ground and V_{out} to smooth the output signal; it will average the signal better.

All sensors have several characteristics, which are quite different, from the theoretical - or maybe expected - behavior. The data sheet for the TMP35/TMP36/TMP37 sensors lists some of these characteristics. You should be mindful, especially when interpreting the results.

12.4.1 Digital to Analog

An essential component of the Arduino board is the digital-to-analog converter (DAC). In this case it is a 10-bit converter, which means that digitally, it can distinguish 2^{10} or 1024 states. If the analog input voltage is referenced at 5 V, it means that the maximum resolution is roughly 5 mV. On the other hand, a 16-bit DAC board would have a resolution of roughly 80 μV, or about 4 significant digits maximally.

Software can easily handle digital information, so sensor's analog output is generally converted into a digital signal, which will be read with the function **analogRead()**, see Listing 12.2. Arduino's DAC outputs a value between 0 and 1023, which must be converted to a voltage. If the reference signal is 5 V, then it is converted with a factor $5/1024$.

Listing 12.2: Arduino code to make readings of the temperature sensor TMP36GZ. The function returns a float value with the temperature in units of °C.

```
   // read out TMP36GZ temperature sensor on analog pin 0
3  float readTMP36GZ()
   {
     float celsius;
     int sensorValue = analogRead(A0);
     // convert DAC to voltage, assuming 5V input
8    float sensorFloat = sensorValue*5.0/1024.0;
     //  Serial.println(sensorFloat, 2);

     // take the average value of 10 readings
     for (int i=2; i <=10; i++) {
13     sensorValue = analogRead(A0);
       sensorFloat += sensorValue*5.0/1024.0;
     }
     sensorFloat /= 10.0;

18   celsius = (sensorFloat - 0.5) * 100.0;
     return celsius;
   }
```

12.4.2 Thermal Characteristics

The temperature sensor will produce heat through common resistive heating, also known as Joule heating. For Joule heating, the heat power generated is $P = I^2 R$, so proportional to the square of the current. Therefore, the sensor (die) will be slightly hotter than the sample (socket) that it is mounted to. In still air - without a fan - this effect is small, or about 0.04 °C at room temperature with a 5 V energy supply. This is smaller than the sensitivity of the sensor.

The transient time, or time to reach equilibrium, is set by the thermal capacities of the sensor (die plus case) and the sample, as well as air surrounding it. In still air, typical relaxation times can be tens of seconds, while in stirred oil, the times can be reduced to a few seconds.

12.4.3 Black Body Radiation

In this experiment, we will examine some principles from the black body radiation. In particular, we will compare aluminum cases of equal mass, but different color and their performance in heating up, as well as giving heat off.

In the first part, we prepare the Arduino board with two temperature sensors that can be read at the same time. One sensor is connected to the darker object, and the other to the lighter object. We will then use

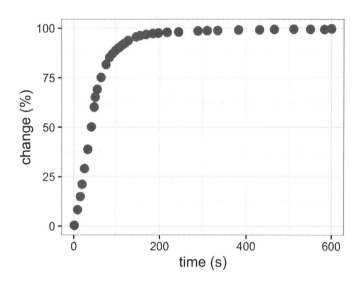

Figure 12.1: Thermal response time for TMP35 SOIC soldered to 0.5" × 0.3" Cu PCB in still air adopted from the data sheet for TMP35/TMP36/TMP37.

a lamp of known power output, measure the distance and compute the incident energy onto the object. Make sure to start the experiment in equilibrium at room temperature, then turn on the light and wait for the new equilibrium temperature. Later analyze the power, and the relaxation time for reaching the higher temperature.

In the second part, start the two objects at the same temperature and let them cool down. Again, monitor carefully the temperature as a function of time as the objects are cooling. Try to also predict which body will cool faster, the darker or lighter body.

12.4.4 Exporting Data in Arduino

If the Arduino board has a WiFi shield attached, then you can send the measurement data directly to a computer that will capture. The basic Arduino, however, communicates via the serial port. The serial port needs to be enabled first with the **Serial.begin** command, see Listing 12.3. You can then use the **Serial.print** to output a number and communicate via USB back to the computer. When you monitor the serial output, you can monitor the signal. Use the copy command and paste the information into a spreadsheet that you can read and analyze within Excel or R.

Listing 12.3: Arduino code to illustrate the use of the serial port for data communication.

```
void setup() {
    // opens serial port, sets data rate to 9600 bps
    Serial.begin(9600);

5   // print header
    Serial.println("time (s), pin 0 (V)");
}

void loop() {
10  // read the analog input on pin 0:
    float analogVolt = analogRead(0)*5.0/1024;

    // print it out in many formats:
    Serial.print(analogVolt);        // print as an ASCII-encoded decimal
15  Serial.print(",");
    Serial.println(analogValue);     // print as an ASCII-encoded decimal

    // delay 100 milliseconds before the next reading:
    delay(100);
20 }
```

12.5 Exp III: Bot

The bot project is really about engineering a robotics device. It also has a challenge, a course will be given that the bot has to navigate. The course is outlined with white tape on a black table surface. The bot has to follow the course and then park in front of a large wood block. Therefore, you should equip your bot with the necessary sensors and program it to complete the task safely.

In addition to the line follow sensor that operates with infrared and detects a change in the contrast on the table, you should also use low-cost ultrasonic distance sensors. Other sensors may also be incorporated. Additionally, you could have LEDs show you feed-back.

The sample program in Listing 12.4 loads functions from the RedBot library. You can install the library, by selecting Sketch → Include Library → Manage Library and search for the SparkFun RedBot Library. Once the library is installed you can use functions such as **motors.drive()**, which will turn on the motors.

Listing 12.4: Arduino code for RedBot.

```
#include <RedBot.h>   // loads RedBot library
// Provides special objects, methods, and functions for the RedBot.

5  RedBotMotors motors;  // Initiate motor controls

void setup()
```

```
{
    motors.drive(127);      // Turn on Left and right motors at half speed.
                            // Max speed is 255
    delay(1000);            // Waits for 1 seconds
    motors.stop();          // Stops both motors
}

void loop()
{
    // Nothing here. We'll get to this in the next experiment.
}
```

12.6 Arduino Lab Report

The lab report includes the results from the first two experiments. This includes a graph of the resistance versus the flex sensors position. In the analysis, you discuss the limitations of the sensor and make a comparison with the available data from the sensor. In the second part, include the results of temperature versus time for heating and cooling two differently colored objects. Discuss the results with your understanding of black body radiation. Discuss the implications of the results on how to color buildings, cars, and so on.

13 Final Project

In the final project, you will design an experiment that extends and includes one of the experimental techniques that you learned. You will perform the experiment and present the results in a presentation. The process is based on the procedure used by the National Science Foundation (NSF), which awards funding to scientists and researcher in the United States of America.

In the first phase, the opportunity for the final project is announced by the instructor. Clear guidelines are given as to what projects will be supported. Based on this solicitation, a proposal is submitted in the form of a short class presentation. Proposal are either accepted or rejected. The proposals should clearly address the motivation and intellectual merit of the experiment.

The proposal outlines all the experimental parts that are needed as well as the method that will be applied to the experiment. Make sure that you can formulate the problem (research question) clearly and describe the purpose. The method would outline the process that you are going to use. Sometimes, you can write out a hypothesis that can be tested, and sometimes there is a prediction. It is important to define the variables of the experiment and think about which variables are independent, dependent, and fixed? Sometimes, innocuous parameters, such as the temperature may need to be fixed for the experiment.

During the performance of the experiment, details need to be recorded meticulously. In the event that experiment does not work as intended, the details will be important in describing what method was used and what outcomes were obtained. Even experiments that seemingly did not end with concrete results contain important information that should be disseminated. For example, a noise level or experimental bound can be discussed.

Importantly, the results and analysis need to be disseminated. Generally, a summary report is written and an oral presentation given to an audience of interested peers. Communication of scientific results is particularly important in light of funding impasses. For a good presentation, you should tell a story to the audience. The slides in the background merely provide pictorial support, rarely should the slides be used for text. Avoid presenting the story in a historical fashion; i.e. presenting your experiment in the way it happened. Rather think of how you can rearrange the events, so that the story has a logical progression. As a first step, make a draft of the narrative on paper or use a whiteboard. Next, print all the graphs, supporting schematics, sketches, and images that you are going to use, make sure that you are not infringing on any copyrights and include annotations, if you are using other people's work. Try to use your own work, photos, and diagrams.

The results will be judged and evaluated by your peers.

In the following a few examples are presented. However, projects that include your own interests, ideas, curiosities, or projects that are related to your thesis work are preferred.

The project should be feasible to be completed within the short period of time, so a good plan at hand is essential. At the forefront of an experiment lies a question. Along with this question, there may be a prediction, or different possibilities of outcomes. The possible results should be carefully planned for and thought through. Equipment and materials need to be available.

Part of the excitement is the planning phase, followed by carrying out the experiment. At the end the results, and analysis of the experiment should be shared in a presentation to an audience. The presentation should not tell the temporal flow of your experiment, but rather follow a logical sequence trying to answer the outstanding question from the beginning.

13.1 AFM projects

- AFM of interdigitated electrodes and measure capacitances with water, methanol, and acetone
- Thickness variations of gold across surface
- Gold annealing study (surface of gold before and after annealing)
- Steel surface analysis
- Nanoparticle analysis
- Taxonomy of Mayflies
- Detect spoiled milk

- Detect alcohols
- Surface roughness of nail polishers
- Differences in roughness

13.2 Lithography projects

- RFID coil
- Limitations of Inkjet photolithography
- Cr mask samples and recipe changes
- Ultimate resolution using different patters
- Effects of contact resistance

13.3 NMR projects

- NMR with Epoxy Cure
- Fourier analysis of the FID signal
- Compare T_1 and T_2 for motor oil, glycerine, and mineral oil.
- Spin relaxation in maple syrup

13.4 Arduino projects

- Ultrasonic range sensor (maxsonar EZ0)
- Speed of sound versus temperature
- Microphone to detect loudness
- Color detector
- Measuring heart rate
- Solar panel response to different LEDs
- Angular dependence of light transmission
- Light attenuation (Beer's Law)

References

Binnig, G., Quate, C. F., & Gerber, C. (1986, March). Atomic Force Microscope. *Physical Review Letters*, *56*(9), 930–933.

Binnig, G., Rohrer, H., Gerber, C., & Weibel, E. (1982, January). Tunneling through a controllable vacuum gap. *Applied Physics Letters*, *40*(2), 178–180.

Bohr, N. (1925, December). Atomic Theory and Mechanics. *Nature*, *116*, 845–852.

Butt, H.-J., Cappella, B., & Kappl, M. (2005, October). Force measurements with the atomic force microscope: Technique, interpretation and applications. *Surface Science Reports*, *59*(1), 1–152.

Carr, H. Y., & Purcell, E. M. (1954, May). Effects of Diffusion on Free Precession in Nuclear Magnetic Resonance Experiments. *Physical Review*, *94*(3), 630–638.

Chen, Y., & Huang, W. (2004). Numerical simulation of the geometrical factors affecting surface roughness measurements by AFM. *Measurement Science and Technology*, *15*(10), 2005.

Dumas, R. K., Gredig, T., Li, C.-P., Schuller, I. K., & Liu, K. (2009, July). Angular dependence of vortex-annihilation fields in asymmetric cobalt dots. *Physical Review B*, *80*(1), 014416.

Duong, K. (2010, December). Rolling Out Zotero Across Campus as a Part of a Science Librarian's Outreach Efforts. *Science & Technology Libraries*, *29*(4), 315–324.

Esposito, W. J., Mujica, F. A., Garcia, D. G., & Kovacs, G. T. A. (2015, August). The Lab-In-A-Box project: An Arduino compatible signals and electronics teaching system. In *2015 IEEE Signal Processing and Signal Processing Education Workshop (SP/SPE)* (pp. 301–306).

Freeman, R. (2003). *Magnetic Resonance in Chemistry and Medicine* (1edition ed.). Oxford ; New York: Oxford University Press.

Gentry, K. P., Gredig, T., & Schuller, I. K. (2009, November). Asymmetric grain distribution in phthalocyanine thin films. *Physical Review B*, *80*(17), 174118.

Giessibl, F. J. (2003, July). Advances in atomic force microscopy. *Reviews of Modern Physics*, *75*(3), 949–983.

Giles, J. (2012, January). Going paperless: The digital lab. *Nature*, *481*(7382), 430–431.

Gredig, T. (1998). *Quantitative magnetic force microscopy with electron beam deposited spike tips* (M.S. Thesis). University of Minnesota, Twin Cities.

Gredig, T., Gentry, K. P., Colesniuc, C. N., & Schuller, I. K. (2010, September). Control of magnetic properties in metallo-organic thin films. *Journal of Materials Science*, *45*(18), 5032–5035.

Gredig, T., Silverstein, E. A., & Byrne, M. P. (2013, March). Height-Height Correlation Function to Determine Grain Size in Iron Phthalocyanine Thin Films. *Journal of Physics: Conference Series*, *417*(1), 012069.

Hahn, E. L. (1950, November). Spin Echoes. *Physical Review*, *80*(4), 580–594.

Harris, R. K. (1986). *Nuclear Magnetic Resonance Spectroscopy*. Burnt Mill, Harlow, Essex, England; New York: Longman Publishing Group.

Horcas, I., Fernández, R., Gómez-Rodríguez, J. M., Colchero, J., Gómez-Herrero, J., & Baro, A. M. (2007, January). WSXM: A software for scanning probe microscopy and a tool for nanotechnology. *Review of Scientific Instruments*, *78*(1), 013705.

Janssen, M., Norton, J. D., Renn, J., Sauer, T., & Stachel, J. (2007). Introduction to Volumes 1 and 2: The Zurich Notebook and the Genesis of General Relativity. In M. Janssen, J. D. Norton, J. Renn, T. Sauer, & J. Stachel (Eds.), *The Genesis of General Relativity* (pp. 7–20). Springer Netherlands.

Kanare, H. M. (1985). *Writing the Laboratory Notebook* (1edition ed.). Washington, D.C: American Chemical Society.

Kirby, K., & Houle, F. A. (2004, November). Ethics and the welfare of the physics profession. *Physics Today*, *57*(11), 42–46.

Klapetek, P., Necas, D., & Anderson, C. (2016). *Gwyddion user guide*. http://gwyddion.net/documentation/user-guide-en/.

Macfarlane, B., & Cheng, M. (2008, March). Communism, Universalism and Disinterestedness: Re-examining Contemporary Support among Academics for Merton's Scientific Norms. *Journal of Academic Ethics*, *6*(1), 67–78.

Mack, C. (2007). *Fundamental Principles of Optical Lithography: The Science of Microfabrication*. Chichester, West Sussex, England ; Hoboken, NJ, USA: Wiley.

Mandelbrot, B. B. (1983). *The fractal geometry of nature*. Macmillan.

Meiboom, S., & Gill, D. (1958, August). Modified Spin-Echo Method for Measuring Nuclear Relaxation Times. *Review of Scientific Instruments*, *29*(8), 688–691.

Merton, R. K. (1996). *On Social Structure and Science* (1st edition ed.; P. Sztompka, Ed.). Chicago: University Of Chicago Press.

Miller, C. W., Chabot, M. D., & Messina, T. C. (2009, December). A student's guide to searching the literature using online databases. *American Journal of Physics*, *77*(12), 1112–1117.

Moore, G. E. (1998, January). Cramming More Components Onto Integrated Circuits. *Proceedings of the IEEE*, *86*(1), 82–85.

Pauli, W. (1925, January). Über den Zusammenhang des Abschlusses der Elektronengruppen im Atom mit der Komplexstruktur der Spektren. *Zeitschrift für Physik*, *31*(1), 765–783.

Proksch, R., Skidmore, G. D., Dahlberg, E. D., Foss, S., Schmidt, J. J., Merton, C., ... Dugas, M. (1996, October). Quantitative magnetic field measurements with the magnetic force microscope. *Applied Physics Letters*, *69*(17), 2599–2601.

Sarik, J., & Kymissis, I. (2010, October). Lab kits using the Arduino prototyping platform. In *2010 IEEE Frontiers in Education Conference (FIE)* (pp. T3C–1–T3C–5).

Schuetze, A. P., Lewis, W., Brown, C., & Geerts, W. J. (2004, February). A laboratory on the four-point probe technique. *American Journal of Physics*, *72*(2), 149–153.

Sedin, D. L., & Rowlen, K. L. (2001, October). Influence of tip size on AFM roughness measurements. *Applied Surface Science*, *182*(1–2), 40–48.

Shor, P. (1997, October). Polynomial-Time Algorithms for Prime Factorization and Discrete Logarithms on a Quantum Computer. *SIAM Journal on Computing*, *26*(5), 1484–1509.

Straumann, N. (2011). Einstein's 'Zurich Notebook' and his Journey to General Relativity. *Annalen Phys.*, *523*, 488–500.

Vandersypen, L. M. K., & Chuang, I. L. (2005, January). NMR techniques for quantum control and computation. *Reviews of Modern Physics*, *76*(4), 1037–1069.

Zahl, P., Bierkandt, M., Schröder, S., & Klust, A. (2003, March). The flexible and modern open source scanning probe microscopy software package GXSM. *Review of Scientific Instruments*, *74*(3), 1222–1227.

Zahl, P., Wagner, T., Möller, R., & Klust, A. (2010, May). Open source scanning probe microscopy control software package GXSM. *Journal of Vacuum Science & Technology B*, *28*(3), C4E39–C4E47.

Index

Acetone, 90
Activity, 26
AFM, 59, 61, 70, 117
Arduino, 93, 129
Atomic Force Microscopy, *see* AFM
Authorship, 8

Bibliography, 25
Bloch Equation, 50
Bohr Magneton, 44
Boltzmann Factor, 45, 48

Cantilever, 62
Carr, 53
Carr-Purcell-Meiboom-Gill, 109
Clean Surfaces, 83
Coarse Approach, 114
Contaminations, 90
Copyright, 8

Data Management Plan, 15
Deuterium, 57
Developer, 87, 88
Double Tip, 64
Duty Cycles, 104
Dynamic Mode, 61, 64, 69

Etching, 88
Ethics, 5

Fair Use, 9

Feedback Loop, 75
FID, 40
Fitting Data, 37
Force Curves, 73
Four-Point Probe, 91
Fourier Transform, 56
Free Induction Decay, 41, 100

Glycerin, 108
Grading Rubric, 34
Grain Size, 119
Gyromagnetic Factor, 44
Gyromagnetic Ratio, 45, 47, 48

Hamaker Constant, 61
Harmonic Oscillator, 64
HDMS, 83
Height-Height Correlation, 119
Hot Plate, 86
Hydrogen Atom, 44

Image Processing, 60, 75, 76, 118
ImageJ, 90, 119, 127
Impact Factor, 22

Lab Notebook, 13, 16, 108
Larmor, 42, 45, 47, 51, 54, 55, 99, 102, 106
Lithography, 81, 90

Magnetic Moment, 43–45

Magnetic Resonance Image, 54
Mask Aligner, 86
MFM, 72
Mineral Oil, 57
MRI, 54, 55

NMR, 51, 99
Non-Contact AFM, 73
Notebook, 13
Nuclear Spin, 41, 44

Open Access Journals, 6
Oscilloscope, 38, 99–108

Pauli, 42
Phase Imaging, 72
Photolithography
    see Lithography 79
Photoresist, 81, 85, 87, 89, 125
PID, 75, 115
Piezo-Electric, 62
Plagiarism, 7
Plasma Etching, 88
Polarization, 49
Post-Bake, 88
Prebake, 86
Precession, 45–47, 50
Publications, 21
Pulsed Nuclear Magnetic Reso-
    nance, 41
Purcell, 53

Quantum Computing, 56

R, 5, 35, 38, 108
Rabi, 42
Radio Frequency Pulses, 51
Raw Data, 2, 3
Refereed Journal, 8
Reference, 25

Relaxation Time, 53
Report Structure, 29
Resonance Frequency, 72
RF Pulse Generator, 102
Roughness, 118
Rubric, 17

Softbake, 86
SOP, 9, 34, 100
Spin Coater, 125
Spin Echo, 53
Spring Constants, 63
Sputtering, 89
Standard Operating Procedure
    see SOP 33
Static Mode, 61, 64, 68
Substrate, 82
Surface Roughness, 118

Temperature Sensor, 132
Thesis, 9, 29
Title, 30
Transparency, 87
Trigger, 101
Tuning, 106

Ultrasonic Bath, 83
Unique File Names, 15

Van Der Pauw Method, 91
Van Der Waals, 60
Voltage Divider, 132

Watershed Algorithm, 119
Web of Science, 27

Young's Modulus, 63

Zotero, 3, 26

Made in the USA
San Bernardino, CA
04 September 2019